TABLE OF CONTENTS

Page

ACRONYMS

CNA	Computer Network Attack
CNCI	Comprehensive National Cybersecurity Initiative
CND	Computer Network Defense
CNE	Computer Network Exploitation
CNO	Computer Network Operations
CO	Cyberspace Operations
CSIS	Center for Strategic and International Studies
DHS	Department of Homeland Security
DIRNSA	Director, National Security Agency/Central Security Service
DOD	Department of Defense
DOJ	Department of Justice
DOS	Department of State
FBI	Federal Bureau of Investigation
HSPD	Homeland Security Presidential Directive
IC	Intelligence Community
IO	Information Operations
IW	Information Warfare
JP	Joint Publication
NCRCG	National Cyber Response Coordination Group
NDS	National Defense Strategy
NMS	National Military Strategy
NMS-CO	National Military Strategy for Cyberspace Operations

NPISP	National Plan for Information Systems Protection
NSA/CSS	National Security Agency/Central Security Service
NSPD	National Security Presidential Directive
NSS	National Security Strategy
PDD	Presidential Decision Directive
QDR	Quadrennial Defense Review
U.S.	United States
USG	United States Government
USSTRATCOM	United States Strategic Command
USCYBERCOM	United States Cyber Command

ILLUSTRATIONS

TABLES

CHAPTER 1

INTRODUCTION

It's now clear this cyber threat is one of the most serious economic and national security challenges we face as a nation. It's also clear that we're not as prepared as we should be, as a government or as a country.

— President Barack Obama,
Remarks by the President on Securing
Our Nation's Cyber Infrastructure

Background

As society becomes more reliant upon computers and their associated technology to facilitate everyday life, to support critical national infrastructure and to enhance communications, the risk of cyber-attack is a significant security concern. *The National Plan for Information Systems Protection* (NPISP) defines critical infrastructure as "Those systems and assets, both physical and cyber, so vital to the Nation that their incapacity or destruction would have a debilitating impact on national security, national economic security, and/or national public health and safety."[1] The banking community, trade (stocks, commodities), power plants and grids, water and sewage treatment facilities, transportation and manufacturing all fall within the scope of this definition, and are susceptible to cyber attack. If a malicious state or non-state actor gained unauthorized access to a company, industry, or large area-wide network's system, they could cause massive confusion, delay, physical damage, and death to the targeted entity.

---

[1]White House, *National Plan for Information Systems Protection Version 1.0: An Invitation to a Dialogue* (Washington, DC: Government Printing Office, 2000), vi.

The decreasing technological and intellectual threshold for engaging in cyber operations continues as the price of cyber-related technology falls. With sophisticated hardware and software becoming more widespread and easier to use, less technically proficient persons or groups have the potential to become more effective at conducting cyber operations. The threat is increasing exponentially, a concept most aptly captured by Moore's Law (by Gordon Moore, co-founder of Intel). Moore's Law predicted, "that the number of transistors on a chip [microprocessor] will double approximately every two years."[2] This rapid growth in microprocessor development grants everyday technology the power of "supercomputers" of old. The United States, however, currently lacks a comprehensive strategy and supporting policies to combat this growing threat.

Additionally, with different authorities and foci stemming from various laws and executive policies, the U.S. cyber organizational structure is decentralized. The current structure is spread across multiple agencies, making coherent and consistent government-wide action challenging. President Obama has bluntly stated, "No single official oversees cybersecurity policy across the federal government, and no single agency has responsibility or authority to match the scope and scale of the challenge. Indeed, when it comes to cybersecurity, federal agencies have overlapping missions and don't coordinate and communicate as well as they should-with each other or with the private sector."[3]

---

[2]Intel, Moore's Law, http://www.intel.com/content/www/us/en/silicon-innovations/moores-law-technology.html (accessed November 12, 2012). Moore's Law Example: In 1970, 2,300 transistors fit on a single microprocessor; in 1980 that number was 134,000; by 2000 that number had grown to 32million; and in 2011it was 1.3billion.

[3]White House, "Remarks by the President on Securing Our Nation's Cyber Infrastructure," http://www.whitehouse.gov/the-press-office/remarks-president-securing-our-nations-cyber-infrastructure (accessed November 19, 2012).

Given these challenges and perceived gaps in cybersecurity, is the United States' cyber organization postured to meet the post-9/11 security environment? Does the interagency division of labor between the Department of Defense (DOD), Department of Homeland Security (DHS), and Department of Justice (DOJ) enhance or weaken U.S. cybersecurity? Should the current interagency division of responsibility be consolidated into either DOD or DHS? In order to respond to these questions adequately, additional questions must be answered. What does the U.S. cyber organization look like and how do its parts and layers interact with one another? What are each agency's roles and responsibilities? What is current U.S. cyber policy and how has it developed over time? How do the current interagency relationships within the U.S. cyber organization compare to other large interagency groups like the Intelligence Community (IC)?

Limitations

Within joint doctrine, Computer Network Operations (CNO) is one of the components of Information Operations (IO). CNO is further divided into three subsets: Computer Network Attack (CNA), Computer Network Defense (CND), and Computer Network Exploitation (CNE). Information on IO and CNO is largely restricted to the classified arena. Given these limitations, specific U.S. cyber capabilities (tools), tactics, techniques, and procedures will not be included in this study. In order to foster increased awareness and discussion of how U.S. cyber policy and its accompanying organizational structure address cyber threats, this research study will only incorporate open source and unclassified aspects of cyber policy and organization.

Delimitations

In determining whether U.S. cyber policy and organizational is properly structured for the post 9/11 security environment, this research study compares and contrasts government entities tasked with cyber security. These agencies include the DHS, DOD, and DOJ. The effectiveness of individual departments in performing their assigned missions is beyond the scope of the research and is not evaluated. The effectiveness of interagency connections between cyber organizations are not judged for the same reason.

In cases involving military cyber capabilities, Joint-service examples illustrate salient points to the greatest extent possible. There are two reasons. First, the executor (or executive agent) of the DOD-wide cyber mission is the United States Cyber Command (USCYBERCOM), a joint service command comprised of elements from all the armed services. Second, discussion at the joint-service level provides a "service neutral" perspective. For those instances where service specific references and comparison are needed, the navy component is used.

As this research study is interested primarily in the defensive and deterrent nature of U.S. cyber policy and organization, Computer Network Defense is the key concern. Computer Network Attack and Computer Network Exploitation will not be covered in depth except as a means to highlight and illustrate points relating to Computer Network Defense and cyber security.

This research relies heavily on national strategy and policy documents. Policies dealing primarily with international relationships and organizations are beyond the purview of this study. Although U.S. cybersecurity strategy and policy consists of both domestic and international components, this research is primarily concerned with the domestic implications and interagency interactions associated with cybersecurity.

Cybersecurity plays a significant role in the protection of the nation's critical infrastructure. Current focus on cybersecurity can be traced to a rising interest in critical infrastructure protection during the Clinton administration. Despite the linkage between infrastructure protection and cyber issues, this research will focus on cybersecurity matters. Critical infrastructure protection is discussed as it applies to cybersecurity strategy, policy, and organization.

Cyber capabilities and U.S. policy are evolving. In order to afford adequate time for document review, critical analysis, data fusion and reporting within the timeframe of the Master's of Military Arts and Sciences program, the information cut-off date was 15 November 2012.

Assumptions

For purposes of this research study, a key assumption is that the 9/11 Commission recommendations corrected the perceived shortcomings of the IC that existed prior to the 9/11 terrorist attack (e.g., stove-piped organizations, poor interagency cooperation). It also assumes that the IC is now agile, response, and pro-active in dealing with threats in the post-9/11 security environment. An additional assumption is that the U.S. cybersecurity organization is similar enough to the IC that these recommendations are appropriate to the former. Both communities span multiple departments and agencies, encompassing defense, intelligence, and law enforcement. This assumption serves as a baseline for comparative analysis of the 9/11 Commission's recommended changes and the degree to which the current cybersecurity organization reflects those suggestions.

Because of the sensitive nature of cyber security data, online data available via open source methods and data available from the private sector is used for illustrative purposes.

Significance

This thesis focuses on U.S. cyber strategy, policy and organization alignment, specifically, DHS, DOD, and DOJ as the country faces an ever-growing cyber threat. It highlights areas of superiority or parity between the current U.S. cyber posture and potential threats, as well as possible vulnerabilities that could make the nation more susceptible to a cyber attack. In order to do this, this study examines the U.S. cyber organization, current and pending strategies, policies and laws, followed by a limited comparative study between U.S. cyber policy/organization and the post-9/11 IC structure. In characterizing the status of the U.S. cyber posture, this study highlights potential gaps or disconnects between policy and organization. Additionally, a lack of organizational flexibility, agility, or responsiveness may pose challenges to military and civilian decision makers as they seek to respond to the growing cyber threat. The study concludes with a determination of whether current cyber strategy, policy, and organization is adequately postured for the post-9/11 security environment or if the United States is potentially vulnerable to a "cyber-9/11" or "cyber-Pearl Harbor" catastrophe.

CHAPTER 2

LITERATURE REVIEW

The prime challenge to analyzing the proposed research question properly is the media used to present the most information on cyber issues. Since internet-based cyber attack is in its relative infancy, there is a limited amount of available literature on cyber issues. As such, most of the information on cyber topics is not available in traditional print form. Instead, the vast majority of material is available on-line via major and minor news outlets, special-interest magazines, trade publications, professional journals, as well as organizational and government websites. While there is no shortage of material in these forums, the challenge is determining which information is credible and useful. The rapidly evolving world of cyberspace adds an additional layer to the challenge of analyzing and synthesizing related documents and publications. For those few authors that have written books on the subject, their theories, assertions and assumptions are also subject to the accelerated evolution of cybersecurity theory and practice.

This research topic focuses on the relationships between organization, strategy and policy. And like the technology that drives cyberspace, that relationship is constantly evolving. As a result, there are few books and monographs relevant to this research. These studies do provide historical context. The literature that is available and useful for this project is categorized into six parts: National Strategy and Policy, Other Strategic Documents, Laws, Directives, and Proposed Legislation, U.S. Cyber Organization, as well as the 9/11 Commission and the IC, Third-party opinion.

The national strategy and policy section examines current national-level strategies and policies. As part of this examination, previous strategies and policies are compared to highlight trends, progress, or stagnation regarding cyber policy. Stand-alone strategic documents and policy reviews are also examined to determine how they augment the primary national security strategic documents (NSS, NDS, and NMS). The laws, directives, and legislation section reviews the existing laws and directives that define current cybersecurity policy. It also reviews proposed cybersecurity laws that Congress recently debated to highlight the pros and cons of those measures. The literature pertaining to the U.S. cyber organization came from government websites (e.g., DOD, DHS) as well as official press releases, speech transcripts and other open-source articles that define the structure of the U.S. cyber enterprise. By studying how the cyber enterprise is organized, one can compare it to the IC. In reviewing IC documentation, specifically the 9/11 Commission findings, a better understanding of the recommended changes that helped correct the perceived faults and failures of the IC is gained. This enables further comparison and analysis of the cyber enterprise and formulation of an answer to the primary research question. Finally, the third-party opinion category includes contributions from think tanks. These contributions include strategy and policy recommendations along with analysis of current strategy and policy documents that provide correlation between the categories and help to answer secondary research questions.

National Strategy and Policy

An examination of how prevalent the term or concept of "cyber" exists within Presidential-level national strategy and the DOD documents provides a notional understanding of how the US government prioritized cyber-related issues. While it does not contain a definition for "cybersecurity," the *DOD Dictionary of Military and*

Associated Terms, contains several "cyber" and cyber-related disciplines. These cyber-references include Computer Network Operations (CNO), Computer Network Attack (CNA), Computer Network Defense (CND), cyberspace operations, cyberspace, and cyber counterintelligence.[4] Additionally, the *National Security Strategy* (NSS), *National Defense Strategy* (NDS), *National Military Strategy* (NMS), and *Quadrennial Defense Review* (QDR) all cite the strategic importance and necessity of protecting friendly cyberspace while denying enemy use of the same. Each of these documents provided a coherent understanding of the challenges and the policy responses to cybersecurity issues. An assessment of these strategic documents helped determine if the USG addressed cyberspace issues in a similar and consistent manner. In sum, a review of the official literature indicates that the USG has treated cyber issues consistently, albeit in very broad terms.

The *Presidential Cyberspace Policy Review* of May 2009, while not strategy per se, makes strong recommendations on actions to correct perceived cyber deficiencies. It also speaks most specifically and candidly about the United States' vulnerabilities and shortcomings in its current policy and capabilities. It has been included in this grouping because it is an executive branch publication similar to other national strategy and policy documents, and it is an executive branch publication. Some of the assertions within this policy review were useful in answering the primary research question. The *National Strategy to Secure Cyberspace* is also included as well as government reports speaking to

---

[4]Chairman, Joint Chiefs of Staff, Joint Publication (JP) 1-02, *Department of Defense Dictionary of Military and Associated Terms* (Washington, DC: Government Printing Office, 2012), 65, 83.

cyber readiness. The latter include such documents as the Federal Emergency Management Agency's 2012 *National Preparedness Report*.

With a 3-7 year gap between publication of the same document, previous editions of the NSS, NDS, and NMS were also examined to determine if any themes or trends were consistently emphasized. Specifically, these documents were reviewed not only to see if "cyber" issues were addressed, but also to discern if substantial progress was made in the newer editions. This analysis helped determine if the USG cyber policy and organizational evolution was relevant to the post-9/11 strategic environment. The articulation of more advanced or refined goals that built upon past successes served as the qualitative assessment of progress. For example, the latest NDS was released in January 2012, while the most recent NSS and NMS were released in May 2010 and February 2011, respectively. The previous editions of these strategies were March 2005 for the NDS, March 2006 for the NSS, 2004 for the NMS, and a special NMS for Cyberspace Operations issued in December 2006. Initially classified at the secret level, this focused NMS on Cyberspace Operations was partially declassified, though significant portions were redacted and remain unavailable at the unclassified level.

These national-level policies are analyzed chronologically to identify progress and trends within the same family of strategies. Each of these strategies is normally "nested" within the foundational NSS. A chronological analysis identified change over time and provided policy continuity or discontinuity within the strategies and associated presidential administrations.

National Defense Strategy

Sustaining U.S. Global Leadership: Priorities for 21st Century Defense is the latest in a long line of national defense strategies. Notable for being about half the size of previous national defense strategies, it is also deals with cyber issues tangentially. It acknowledges, "Both state and non-state actors possess the capability and intent to conduct cyber espionage and, potentially, cyber attacks on the United States, with possible severe effects on both our military operations and our homeland."[5] In order to deal with this cyber threat, this strategy calls for DOD to "invest in advanced capabilities to defend its networks, operational capability, and resiliency in cyberspace and space."[6] Its lengthier predecessor, the 2008 NDS is notable for two items that were not included in the *Priorities for 21st Century Defense*. While DOD may be called upon to "respond to protect lives and national assets" in the event of a cyber-attack, the NDS concluded "in the long run the DOD is neither the best source of resources and capabilities nor the appropriate authority to shoulder these tasks."[7] The second difference highlighted the growing risk that China poses as it develops its cyber warfare capability.[8]

---

[5]Department of Defense, *Sustaining U.S. Global Leadership: Priorities for 21st Century Defense* (Washington, DC: Government Printing Office, 2012), 3.

[6]Ibid., 5.

[7]Department of Defense, *National Defense Strategy* (Washington, DC: Government Printing Office, 2008), 7.

[8]Ibid., 22.

National Military Strategy

The most current NMS includes cyberspace as part of the "global commons," a term that has historically been used to describe the maritime domain, but has been expanded to include air and space. Similar to the 2008 NDS, the 2011 NMS speaks of the growing risk of cyber attacks, and while it does not attribute that risk to a specific country as the NDS did to China, the NMS acknowledged, "Some states are conducting or condoning cyber intrusions that foreshadow the growing threat in this globally connected domain."[9] In order to counter this threat, the NMS stated that DOD "will enhance deterrence in air, space, and cyberspace by possessing the capability to fight through a degraded environment and improving our ability to attribute and defeat attacks on our systems or supporting infrastructure."[10] The core mission of the armed forces is "to defend our Nation and win its wars." To defeat aggression, the armed forces must "integrate core military competencies across all domains." This includes "the ability to maintain joint assured access to the global commons and cyberspace should they become contested, and the ability to fight and win against adversaries."[11] The 2004 NMS referred to the cyberspace domain as part of the battle space and that military capabilities must guarantee access.[12]

---

[9]Chairman, Joint Chiefs of Staff, *The National Military Strategy of the United States of America* (Washington, DC: Government Printing Office, 2011), 3.

[10]Ibid., 8.

[11]Ibid., 8-9.

[12]Chairman, Joint Chiefs of Staff, *The National Military Strategy of the United States of America* (Washington, DC: Government Printing Office, 2004), 18.

National Security Strategy

The NSS is the nation's overarching strategic document. The NDS and NMS supplement the NSS. Each of the former is generally more specific in how it supports the NSS goals. Several earlier editions were also used in determining if the NSS was evolving with respect to cybersecurity policy and strategy.

While published prior to the 2011 NMS and 2012 NDS, the NSS's "Secure Cyberspace" section provides more detail than the NMS or NDS.[13]

U.S. Cyber Organization

The DHS continues to assert primacy in most areas of national cyber security. By law and presidential directive, DHS is the lead agency for cybersecurity. However, DOD and DOJ, specifically the Federal Bureau of Investigation (FBI), also have major roles to play. National cyber security naturally involves DOD, DOJ, and DHS, but each has a different mandate to fulfill. Despite the established "supported vs. supporting" roles, the extent to which DHS or DOD attains primacy in practice remains unanswered. The existing cybersecurity connections between DHS, DOD, and DOJ provide an adequate starting point to analyzing the interagency dynamics regarding cyber organization and policy.

Laws, Directives, and Proposed Legislation

Several laws and directives were reviewed to understand the cybersecurity legal landscape. Examining these documents revealed the lead departments and agencies for

---

[13]White House, *National Security Strategy* (Washington, DC: Government Printing Office, 2010), 27.

national cybersecurity. *The Homeland Security Act of 2002* established DHS as the cybersecurity lead, with DOD, DOJ and the remaining federal departments as supporting members. HSPDs 5 and 7 expand upon the role of DHS in protecting the nation's critical infrastructure and serve to establish how several departments support this mission.

Congress has recently considered legislation that would have led to the nation's first robust cyber security law. These bills included the *Cyber Intelligence Sharing and Protection Act (CISPA), Strengthening and Enhancing Cybersecurity by Using Research, Education, Information, and Technology Act of 2012 (SECURE IT)* and the *Cybersecurity Act of 2012*. Debate on these bills involved normal partisan rancor, but also included concerns from citizens regarding privacy concerns. Despite administration support for cybersecurity legislation, all of these bills were defeated. As a result, the Obama administration is contemplating issuing a cybersecurity executive order. The difficulty in passing a comprehensive cybersecurity law highlights the complexity of the cybersecurity problem.

The 9/11 Commission and the Intelligence Community

The 9/11 Commission Report: Final Report of the National Commission on Terrorist Attacks Upon the United States serves as the basis for the comparison and analysis of the cybersecurity organization and the IC. The 9/11 Commission's findings regarding the IC leadership, organization, and functions provide a baseline to assess cyber policy and organizational preparedness. The commission provided many recommendations to improve the IC and to correct perceived deficiencies. Since the IC and cybersecurity organization share similar functional and structural traits, many of the 9/11 Commission recommendations can be applied to the cybersecurity organization. The

IC recommendations are assessed to determine if they would benefit current cybersecurity organization. Fundamentally, can or should cybersecurity organization adopt lessons learned from post-9/11 IC or is the USG repeating past errors that could make the US vulnerable to a cyber-9/11.

Third-party Opinion

This section is concerned with the contributions that third-party organizations, such as think tanks, have made to the national discussion on cybersecurity. Some, like the Center for Strategic and International Studies (CSIS) have even been invited to participate in the formulation of presidential cyber policy. CSIS' primary contributions have been captured within *Securing Cyberspace for the 44th Presidency* and *Cybersecurity Two Years Later*. Others, like the Atlantic Council, charter new ground within the cybersecurity dialogue, focusing on courses of action not previously offered. Their document, *Cyber Security: An Integrated Government Strategy for Progress* is an example of this.

CSIS and the Atlantic Council approach the challenge of cybersecurity differently. While each is professedly non-partisan, their approaches to federal involvement in cybersecurity, specifically federally mandated measures, appeal to different sides of the political aisle. Both perspectives contain measured approaches to cybersecurity and are worthy subjects for this research.

CHAPTER 3

RESEARCH METHODOLOGY

Is American cyber organization and policy postured to meet the post-9/11 security environment? This research project employs a qualitative analysis and comparison of recent and current national policy documents and organizational structures to determine in the United States is prepared to withstand a large-scale cyber attack similar to the Japanese attack at Pearl Harbor or the more recent 9/11 attack on the World Trade Center. The analysis and conclusions are based on:

1. A comparison of national strategy and policies regarding cybersecurity to include:

    a. Self-imposed mission to secure critical infrastructure, global commons of cyberspace.

    b. Self-characterization of USG capacity and capability to secure cyber domain.

    c. Consistency of cybersecurity strategy and policy messaging between strategic documents.

    d. Qualitative evidence of progress between editions of the same strategic documents.

    e. Qualitative evidence of progress among all national strategy documents, laws, and directives.

2. Third party analysis of USG effectiveness in cyber strategy, policy and organization.

3. A comparison of current DHS, DOD and DOJ cyber organization.

a. Characterization of interagency cooperation-evidence of strong, weak, or inefficient cooperation on cybersecurity issues.

b. Does current policy and organization allow cyber enterprise to be flexible and agile in response to current and future threats?

c. Does current organizational construct allow for rapid information dissemination and unity of effort in responding to threats?

4. Identifying cybersecurity limitations

a. Authorities vested in different organizations and departments.

b. Proposed federal legislation.

5. Comparing the current cyber structure to the 9/11 Commission's recommendations for IC reform.

The research culminates in an analysis of the how well the U.S. cybersecurity organization is postured for success in a post-9/11 security environment.

Availability of strategic policy and organizational structures regarding cybersecurity is limited due to security classifications and operational restrictions. This topic will only cover those areas available through open source methods.

The research is organized into three parts. The first focuses on current cyber strategy and policies at the national level. This consists mainly of executive-level documents that establish US cyber structure and policy guidelines and goals. By studying these documents, a qualitative judgment on progress in the cybersecurity arena is made. Cybersecurity is dynamic arena. One would expect strategy and policy to have iterative changes over time. If cybersecurity thought and processes are maturing from one strategy to the next, then follow-on strategies should build upon past successes or focus on new aspects of the cybersecurity challenge. Conversely, if no progress or advancement in strategy and policy occur, then one could expect the strategy to remain the same.

Second, the US cyber organization is studied to understand the extensiveness of its interagency connections. An agile and responsive cyber organization would be replete with these connections, demonstrating cooperation in tackling the cybersecurity problem.

The third part assesses the 9/11 Commission recommendations for IC reform in relation to the current cybersecurity organization. This comparison helps determine if the cybersecurity organization is structured to take advantage of the lessons learned post-9/11 or if the cybersecurity organization more closely resembles the pre-9/11 IC.

The results of this three-part examination are then analyzed. Based upon the results, this study determines if the current cybersecurity organization and policy is postured for success in a post-9/11 security environment or if the US is potentially vulnerable to a devastating cyber attack.

CHAPTER 4

FINDINGS AND ANALYSIS

No single official oversees cybersecurity policy across the federal government,
and no single agency has responsibility or authority to match the scope and scale
of the challenge. Indeed, when it comes to cybersecurity, federal agencies have
overlapping missions and don't coordinate and communicate as well as they
should-with each other or with the private sector.
— President Barack Obama,
Remarks by the President on Securing
Our Nation's Cyber Infrastructure

This study determines whether US cyber policy and organization is properly

postured to deal with a post-9/11 security environment. To accomplish this goal, the

chapter evaluates national strategy and policy documents and it examines current laws

and proposed legislation that affect cybersecurity. Together, these areas provide insight

into how the US government approaches cybersecurity. Next, the U.S. cybersecurity

organization is described. The three key cyber security organizations are DOD, DHS, and

DOJ. Linkages between these and other federal agencies are also examined. This chapter

also compares the post-9/11 IC with the current US cybersecurity organization. The

comparison determines if today's cybersecurity organization can function efficiently,

without the structural stovepipes or bureaucratic impediments that prevent effective

coordination. Finally, this study makes a determination on whether U.S. cybersecurity

policy and organization is postured to deal with the post-9/11 security environment.

National Strategy and Policy

The most significant research challenge was an analysis of the various USG

strategic policy documents. While the genesis of many of these documents was the

Goldwater-Nichols Department of Defense Reorganization Act of 1986, the breadth and depth of US strategy and policy is not limited to just the NSS, NDS, NMS or QDR. There are presidential directives and other related plans and strategies like the *National Plan for Information Systems Protection* that are important to understanding the development of U.S. cybersecurity policy. The majority of documents covered, such as the NSS, NDS, NMS, and QDR, is issued in accordance with congressionally mandated timelines and have had multiple iterations since 9/11. Additionally, these documents encompass multiple presidential administrations. Each placed a different emphasis on the cyber security realm. Some special strategies, such as the *National Security Strategy to Secure Cyberspace*, have been issued in response to growing interest on cyber issues. They are stand-alone documents and do not permit a comparative study. Still other executive branch level cyber focused papers, such as the *Comprehensive National Cybersecurity Initiative* and *Cyberspace Policy Review* are more policy oriented, but they also contain strategic elements relevant to this discussion. This research emphasizes those documents issued since 2001 to evaluate how they influenced US cyber strategy and policy in a post-9/11 security environment.

International strategies and policies such as the *International Strategy for Cyberspace* are not addressed in detail. While the nature of a worldwide internet creates both domestic and international components to cybersecurity, this research project is focused on the interplay of domestic strategy, policy and interagency coordination.

The national strategy documents were analyzed chronologically and conceptually; they were categorized as either "nested" or "familial." The primary national security documents (NSS, NDS, NMS, and QDR) are all nested. Each document is informed by a higher-level document. The QDR is an exception because it informs both the NDS and NMS. This chronological approach provided a snapshot of cybersecurity policy within a 2-3 year period when all the aforementioned documents would be issued. The second category compared these documents to similar documents within a family. Evaluating how NSS documents addressed cyber security issues over time provided insight into the relative priority of cyber issues during and between administrations. The core task in studying national strategy documents was to establish what, if any, focus was placed on cyber issues and identify what, if any, "progress" was made either between nested groups or within familial groups. As quantitative data is limited, progress is assessed subjectively based on an analysis of each document's narrative.

The Obama administration emphasized cybersecurity in its *Cyberspace Policy Review* and subsequent *Comprehensive National Cybersecurity Initiative*. The latter document evolved from a George W. Bush Administration program of the same name, which was contained within NSPD-54/HSPD-23, *Cyber Security and Monitoring, January 2008*. The Obama administration's *Comprehensive National Cybersecurity Initiative* is an unclassified document that updates the public on the cyber initiatives and directives carried over from the Bush administration's Comprehensive National Cybersecurity Initiative. With the exception of what is contained in the *Comprehensive National Cybersecurity Initiative,* NSPD-54/HSPD-23 remains classified. For this discussion, "Comprehensive National Cybersecurity Initiative" refers to both the Obama administration document and NSPD-54/HSPD-23.

Cyberspace as a Domain–The Clinton Administration

While this research emphasizes post-9/11 policies, there was more than just a nascent awareness of the growing importance of cyberspace and its relationship to critical national infrastructure prior to 9/11. In order to understand future national strategy documents, it is important to address the initial directives and documents that were responsible for the government's rising interest in cybersecurity.

The mid-1990s were important in the evolution of American strategic awareness of cyberspace. Presidential Decision Directive-39, *United States Policy on Counterterrorism*, issued in June 1995, was the first strategic document to stress cybersecurity.[14] Even though it remains classified, small excerpts are available through other unclassified documents. Through PDD-39, Clinton tasked the Attorney General to study and report on the vulnerability of the nation's critical infrastructure. The report indicated that the nation was giving insufficient attention to protecting its cyber infrastructure.[15]

Because of the Attorney General's findings, Clinton issued Executive Order 13010, establishing the President's Commission on Critical Infrastructure Protection (PCCIP) to further study the nation's critical infrastructure.[16] The Commission's membership consisted of representatives from government agencies, industry, and

---

[14]White House, Presidential Decision Directive (PDD)-39, *United States Policy on Counterterrorism* (Washington, DC: Government Printing Office, 1995).

[15]White House, *National Plan for Information Systems Protection Version 1.0: An Invitation to a Dialogue* (Washington, DC: Government Printing Office, 2000), xviii.

[16]White House, Executive Order 13010, *Critical Infrastructure Protection* (Washington, DC: Government Printing Office, 1996), 2.

academia (see table 12).[17] The PCCIP provided additional insight into national

infrastructure vulnerabilities. The commission's recommendations for improving

American cybersecurity are found in its 1997 report, *Critical Foundations – Protecting*

America's Infrastructures: The Report of the President's Commission on Critical

Infrastructure Protection. The growing dependence of the nation's critical infrastructure

on cyberspace, and the observation that the public and private sectors were both

responsible for cybersecurity were key findings. "National defense is no longer the

exclusive preserve of government, and economic security is no longer just about

business."[18] The Commission also determined that cyber attacks did not have the

capacity to have a "debilitating effect on the nation's critical infrastructures."[19] On the

other hand, the capacity for cyber attacks to cause harm "is real; it is growing at an

alarming rate; and we have little defense against it."[20] The former point is intriguing

because it describes the same complex problem, integrating the private and public sectors

in the pursuit of greater cybersecurity that exists today.

Based upon both the Attorney General's and PCCIP's findings, President Clinton

issued Presidential Decision Directive-63 (PDD-63), *Critical Infrastructure Protection* in

May 1998. The verbiage in PDD-63 was used by some later strategic policy documents.

---

[17]Chairman, President's Commission on Critical Infrastructure Protection, *Critical Foundations: Protecting America's Infrastructure-The Report of the President's Commission on Critical Infrastructure Protection* (Washington, DC: Government Printing Office, 1997), iii.

[18]Ibid., ix.

[19]Ibid., i.

[20]Ibid.

Ironically, the problems originating from cyberspace and goals for improving national cybersecurity have not changed 14 years after PDD-63's release.[21]

PDD-63 identified American economic power and the US as increasingly vulnerable to malicious actors. The increasing reliance of cyber infrastructures was the major concern with both. To mitigate this growing threat, PDD-63 recommended that the US "take all necessary measures to swiftly eliminate any significant vulnerability to both physical and cyber attacks on our critical infrastructures, especially our cyber systems."[22] The directive identified specific cyber goals and timelines:

> No later than the year 2000, the United States shall have achieved an initial operating capability and no later than five years from today [May 22, 1998] the United States shall have achieved and shall maintain the ability to protect the nation's critical infrastructures from intentional acts that would significantly diminish the abilities of:
>
> 1) The Federal Government to perform essential national security missions and to ensure the general public health and safety;
> 2) State and local governments to maintain order and to deliver minimum essential public services;
> 3) The private sector to ensure the orderly functioning of the economy and the delivery of essential telecommunications, energy, financial and transportation services.
>
> Any interruptions or manipulations to these critical functions must be brief, infrequent, manageable, geographically isolated and minimally detrimental to the welfare of the United States.[23]

PDD-63 was the first document to identify specific sectors that comprise critical infrastructures: "information and communications, energy, banking and finance,

---

[21]White House, Presidential Decision Directive (PDD)-63, *Critical Infrastructure Protection* (Washington, DC: Government Printing Office, 1998).

[22]Ibid.

[23]Ibid.

transportation, water supply, emergency services, and public health, as well as those authorities responsible for the continuity of federal, state, and local governments." The sector-specific nature of critical infrastructure is a concept evolved in later documents.[24] The document also established lead agencies for these specific national infrastructure sectors. PDD-63 reiterated the PCCIP finding that the USG cannot be a single-source solution for national cybersecurity and that the public and private sector must collaborate. Sector specific leads, and public and private sector partnerships, are stressed with minimal changes in the December 2003 Homeland Security Presidential Directive-7 (HSPD-7), *Critical Infrastructure Identification, Prioritization, and Protection.*[25] Other ideas that were developed in later directives included a formal group to foster interagency coordination and a national center to warn of infrastructure attacks.

Defending America's Cyberspace – National Plan for Information Systems Protection Version 1.0: An Invitation to a Dialogue (NISP) appeared in 2000. Like the preceding PCCIP and PDD-63, the document argued that government could not be a single source solution for the nation's cybersecurity. But this document went further stating the need for public and private sector collaboration and cooperation. President Clinton concluded, "We cannot mandate our goal through Government regulation. Each sector must decide for itself what practices, procedures, and standards are necessary for it

---

[24]Ibid.

[25]White House, Homeland Security Presidential Directive (HSPD)-7, *Critical Infrastructure Identification, Prioritization, and Protection* (Washington, DC: Government Printing Office, 2003).

to protect its key systems."[26] Clinton defined the Federal Government's role as the leader in computer security research and development, education, and partner to private sector efforts.[27] Moreover, this document repeated the ambitious goals and timelines established in PDD-23. Unfortunately, the document did not explain how it planned to achieve its goals without centralized control or regulation of the process to improve cybersecurity in both the public and private sectors.

This document also provided early glimpses of the government's understanding of the cyber threat. Richard A. Clarke, the National Coordinator for Security, Infrastructure Protection, and Counter-Terrorism, theorized that America's infrastructure could be the target of a future cyber attack. He stated, "We know other governments are developing that capability," but does not attribute threats to specific countries, or provide evidence backing his assertion.[28] While calling for swift action to meet the PDD-63 timelines, Clarke repeated Clinton's assertion that the President and Congress "cannot and should not dictate solutions for private sector systems."[29]

The NPISP was the first document to define "critical infrastructure." It defined it as "those systems and assets-both physical and cyber-so vital to the Nation that their

---

[26]White House, *National Plan for Information Systems Protection*, iii. This conclusion will be later contested by President Obama as his administration considered a cybersecurity executive order to compensate for Congress' inability to pass comprehensive federal cybersecurity legislation.

[27]Ibid.

[28]Ibid., iv.

[29]Ibid.

incapacity or destruction would have a debilitating impact on national security, national economic security, and/or national public health and safety."[30]

The NPISP also revealed that the Office of Management and Budget (OMB) possessed several statutory responsibilities for managing USG computer security and information technology as well as setting security policy for automated USG computer systems (see table 1).[31] This was significant because there are no established "leads" for cybersecurity and no movement to consolidate or change responsibilities among government agencies prior to the NPISP.

Table 1. Office of Management and Budget's Federal Computer Security and Information Resources Management Responsibilities	
Issue and Focus	**Authorities**
Computer Security and Privacy – Ensure public access to data	Computer Security Act of 1987
Performance and Results – Manage Agency performance of mission, including performance of its practices	Government Performance and Results Act of 1993
Efficiency – Maximizing the use of information collected; minimizing the public burden for data requested	Paperwork Reduction Act of 1996
Agency responsibility to manage Information Technology – procurement, investment, security. Creates CIO position within each Agency	Clinger-Cohen Act of 1996
OMB implements these core principles through recommendations and oversight of the CIO Council	Executive Order 13011

Source: White House, *National Plan for Information Systems Protection Version 1.0: An Invitation to a Dialogue* (Washington, DC: Government Printing Office, 2000), x.

---

[30]Ibid., vi.

[31]Ibid., x.

Ultimately, the NPISP offered a strategic blueprint for securing the nation's information systems. In the process of reconciling ends, ways, and means, NPISP's goal (End) is divided into three approaches (Ways): (1) Prepare and Prevent; (2) Detect and Respond; and (3) Build a Strong Foundation.[32] Furthermore, each approach is subdivided into different programs (Means) (see table 2). Both "Prepare and Prevent" along with "Detect and Respond" continued to appear in later documents. "Build Strong Foundations" related items were also mentioned in later documents; however, they were less frequent, indicating less focus was placed on this approach. The needed emphasis on people, for example (Program 7), which Clarke termed the *"sine qua non"* or essential ingredient to successful cybersecurity does not appear to be realized until more than a decade later.[33] The lack of emphasis on personnel in the intervening years since NPISP may be due to the relative infancy of the internet and cyberspace during the time of its writing. It is not until 2010, for instance, that individual services, such as the navy and air force, emphasized the need for specialized "cyber" personnel through the creation of cyber warfare specialties. Other items such as legislation (Program 9) remained in limbo. Several bills were proposed, but none received enough bipartisan support to become law.

---

[32]Ibid., xi.

[33]Ibid., v.

Table 2.	National Plan for Information Systems Protection
Prepare and Prevent	Those steps which are necessary to minimize the possibility of a significant and successful attack on our critical information networks, and build an infrastructure that remains effective in the face of such attacks. **Program 1**: Identify Critical Infrastructure Assets and Shared Interdependencies and Address Vulnerabilities
Detect and Respond	Those actions required identifying and assessing an attack in a timely way, and then to contain the attack, quickly recover from it, and reconstitute affected systems. **Program 2**: Detect Attacks and Unauthorized Intrusions **Program 3**: Develop Robust Intelligence and Law Enforcement Capabilities to Protect Critical Information Systems, Consistent with the Law **Program 4**: Share Attack Warnings and Information in a Timely Manner **Program 5**: Create Capabilities for Response, Reconstitution, and Recovery
Build Strong Foundations	The things we must do as a Nation to create and nourish the people, organizations, laws, and traditions which will make us better able to Prepare and Prevent, Detect and Respond to attacks on our critical information networks. **Program 6**: Enhance Research and Development in Support of Programs 1-5 **Program 7**: Train and Employ Adequate Numbers of Information Security Specialists **Program 8**: Outreach to Make Americans Aware of the Need for Improved Cyber-Security **Program 9**: Adopt Legislation and Appropriations in Support of Programs 1-8 **Program 10**: In Every Step and Component of the Plan, Ensure the Full Protection of American Citizens' Civil Liberties, Their Rights to Privacy, and Their Rights to the Protection of Proprietary Data

Source: White House, *National Plan for Information Systems Protection* (Washington, DC: Government Printing Office, 2000), xi-xii.

The national security document chart below (see table 3), demonstrates the disjointed timeline associated with the release of national strategy documents. While federal law mandates when these documents are published, some documents, such as the NSS, are issued on an as needed basis. The Clinton Administration, for instance, issued a National Security Strategy in seven of its eight years in power (1994-98 and 2000-01). The George W. Bush Administration did not release a NSS until almost two years in office and only updated it once (at the beginning of the second term). The Obama Administration did not release a NSS until 18 months into its term and has not updated it since.

Table 3. U.S. National Strategy Documents by 1997-2012				
Administration	Quadrennial Defense Review (QDR)	National Security Strategy (NSS)	National Defense Strategy (NDS)	National Military Strategy (NMS)
Clinton	1997	1997	-	1997
Clinton	-	1998	-	-
Clinton	-	2000	-	-
Clinton	-	2001	-	-
Bush	2001	2002	2005	2004
Bush	2006	2006	2008	N/A
Obama	2010	2010	2012*	2011

*Note: *Sustaining U.S. Global Leadership: Priorities for 21ˢᵗ Century Defense* fills DOD guidance piece historically provided by the National Defense Strategy (NDS)

Source: Compiled by author.

NSS 1997–QDR 1997–NMS 1997

It is rare for three of the four documents discussed in this section to be issued in the same year. Since these documents are nested, the NSS normally informs the NDS, which in turn guides the NMS. The QDR influences both the NDS and NMS. This type of sequence normally results in some chronological spacing between documents. However, since these documents were likely drafted in parallel, this provides an excellent opportunity to see if they share ideas, concepts, and concerns about cybersecurity. In particular, the NSS, which was in its fourth iteration of the Clinton Administration, came two years after PDD-39. While important documents such as the PCCIP report and PDD-63 were not released until after the NSS was published (4 and 12 months respectively), one would expect cybersecurity to be included as a topic of interest in the NSS, and perhaps in the QDR and NMS as well.

1997 National Security Strategy

In lieu of the word "cyber," the NSS identified the need to invest in and protect its information infrastructure and information systems (Just one of the categories mentioned earlier). It called on the intelligence community to identify threats to information systems and it argued that defense of these systems was important to maintaining national security.[34] This forward-looking posture is consistent with the Clinton administration's aggressive stance on cybersecurity. Additional development of these cyber-related concepts would be evident in future NSS editions.

1997 Quadrennial Defense Review

The QDR also stressed the need for cybersecurity. Again, the terms used in the document do not include "cyber," but revolve around the military concepts of information warfare (IW) and information operations (IO). Both IW and IO encompass CNO, a joint doctrinal term that includes CAN, CND, and CNE (see glossary). The QDR acknowledged that computer based attacks on the nation's infrastructure was a growing threat. DOD must respond and protect that critical infrastructure.[35] The QDR emphasized that "an information defense system to protect our globally distributed communications and processing network from interference or exploitation by an adversary" was one of

---

[34]White House, *A National Security Strategy for a New Century* (Washington, DC: Government Printing Office, 1997), 18.

[35]Department of Defense, *Report of the Quadrennial Defense Review* (Washington, DC: Government Printing Office, 1997), 28.

five components of DOD's future C4ISR architecture.[36] While understandably focused on military readiness, it also has domestic implications since most DOD information systems reside within the continental United States. These systems are tied to domestic telecommunications systems that PDD-63 identified as part of the nation's critical infrastructure.

Rather than being focusing exclusively on a military solution to military problems, the QDR echoes the need for the DOD to work outside the normal defense apparatus. This effort required cooperation with other federal agencies, allies and private industry in order to defend against hostile information operations. Collaboration with the PCCIP in order to foster those connections was important.[37] The QDR went beyond cooperation and collaboration. "Capabilities to protect information systems must also extend beyond traditional military structures into areas of civilian infrastructure that support national security requirements, such as the telecommunication and air traffic control systems."[38] While visionary, this statement was somewhat controversial. There was no mention of a lead agency/department or discussion on the authorities necessary to execute such action. The question surrounding how civilian and military architectures could be linked to provide improved cybersecurity would come up again in later years, but this QDR made no further recommendations on how or when such linkages should be created and used. Consideration of the legal implications of this idea was also conspicuously absent.

---

[36]Ibid., 70.

[37]Ibid., 87.

[38]Ibid., 88.

1997 National Military Strategy

The NMS reiterates the QDR's concerns, specifically the need to protect America's critical infrastructure. It also mentioned the need to conduct offensive and defensive information operations successfully. The NMS also stated that joint doctrine for information operations was under development. While the NMS offered no clues on this doctrine, it stated that it would "assign appropriate responsibilities to all agencies and commands."[39] Congruent with the QDR's vague reference to intertwining civilian and military architectures, the NMS hinted that command and control of IO would be a joint venture between the military and other agencies, and not solely the responsibility of the military.

NSS 1998–NSS 1999–NSS 2000

The next three iterations of the NSS appeared in 1998, 1999, and 2000 (the Clinton Administration did not issue a NSS 2001). There were no new QDRs, NDSs, or NMSs during this timeframe, so these three NSSs are analyzed as a group.

1998 National Security Strategy

A National Security Strategy for a New Century expands upon the themes and messages in the 1997 version, dedicating a subsection to protecting critical infrastructures from physical and information [cyber] attacks.[40] It mentioned a National Infrastructure Protection Center (NIPC) as a "national focal point for gathering information on threats

---

[39]Chairman, Joint Chiefs of Staff, *The National Military Strategy of the United States of America* (Washington, DC: Government Printing Office, 1997), 25.

[40]White House, *A National Security Strategy for a New Century* (Washington, DC: Government Printing Office, 1998), 20.

to infrastructure." It elaborated, "The NIPC will also coordinate the federal government's response to an incident, including mitigation, investigation and monitoring reconstruction efforts."[41] The NIPC is an important concept since it addresses the issue of "who" will manage the government's situational awareness and response to a crisis. Originally located with the FBI, the NIPC was an interagency entity with private sector involvement. After the DHS was created, the NIPC transitioned to that department's National Protection and Program's Directorate and was renamed the National Infrastructure Coordinating Center (NICC).

1999 National Security Strategy

The 1999 edition of the NSS, *A National Security Strategy for a New Century*, shares the title of its predecessor but the content differs slightly. Rather than having its own sub-section, this document includes "Critical Infrastructure Protection" within the "Defending the Homeland" sub-section. No new concepts, ideas, or policy were introduced, although a small paragraph lists many cybersecurity initiatives discussed in previous documents as ongoing. Of interest, however, was the comment that "Every Federal Department is also developing a plan to protect its own critical infrastructures, which include both cyber and physical dimensions."[42] This is noteworthy because it appears to be an odd, if not confusing next step in increasing federal cybersecurity activity. Since the 1998 NSS detailed the NIPC as manager and focal point for the government's situational awareness and response, one might expect the government to

---

[41]Ibid.

[42]White House, *A National Security Strategy for a New Century* (Washington, DC: Government Printing Office, 1999), 18.

establish a unified approach to protecting its critical infrastructure. Allowing each federal department to establish its own security measures invited uncertainty and mirrored the diversity of private sector approaches.

2000 National Security Strategy

A National Security Strategy for a Global Age added little to the overall cybersecurity discussion; however, a few items are worth noting. The term "cyber" appears more frequently. While not the first time the Clinton administration used the term, increased usage of cyber was directly linked to the growing importance of the internet. Critical infrastructure became more reliant on information systems. Clinton's remarks in the preface hinted at the first-ever national strategy for cybersecurity. While such as strategy was under development, it did not become a reality until the Bush administration issued *The National Strategy to Secure Cyberspace* in February 2003. The NSS also referenced potential cyber conflicts between China and Taiwan, using that scenario as an example of an asymmetric threat to the United States.[43] NSS 2000 also notes that the NIPC had successfully provided warnings on threats to infrastructure and has coordinated numerous cyber attack investigations. No real success stories are cited, but the mention of NIPC within the NSS is indicative that it functioned as desired.

A Post-9/11 World–The Bush Administration

The momentum generated in the cyber arena during the Clinton Administration was dramatically slowed during the Bush Administration, another casualty of the terrorist

---

[43] White House, *A National Security Strategy for a Global Age* (Washington, DC: Government Printing Office, 2000), 31.

attacks of 9/11. Whereas the Clinton Administration was attentive to a variety of security issues across numerous fronts, the Bush Administration focused understandably on counterterrorism and the American-led wars in Afghanistan and Iraq. While cyber does not completely disappear from the national strategic discussion, little "progress" was made relative to the Clinton Administration's policy initiatives.

QDR 2001–NSS 2002–NDS 2005–NMS 2004

The first Bush Administration saw an update to all national strategic documents (QDR, NSS, NDS, and NMS). The NDS was released in March 2005, but was likely drafted the year prior.

2001 Quadrennial Defense Review

The September 2001 QDR served as the first major policy document in this quartet of strategic documents. Cyber is mentioned four times in the 79-page document, but only in very broad terms. Written more than a decade ago, the QDR correctly foreshadowed the possibility of cyber actions within the IO realm. Specifically, the QDR spoke to "Technological advances create the potential that competitions will develop in space and cyber space." It also emphasized an "Increasing potential for miscalculation and surprise."[44] The QDR avoided speculating on the scope or impact these cyber actions might have, but it acknowledged that risks involved with cyber warfare are not fully understood, thereby reducing the ability of the US to manage those risks.[45]

---

[44]Department of Defense, *Quadrennial Defense Review Report* (Washington, DC: Government Printing Office, 2001), 7.

[45]Ibid., 13.

36

2002 National Security Strategy

One would expect subsequent national strategy documents to expand upon cyber operations as a potential threat given the QDR's emphasis on these issues. To the contrary, the September 2002 NSS did not mention cyber, computer security, or even the internet. Instead, the NSS contained vague references to "technology." Terrorism was the primary focus. Given the NSS's overall context, these references to technology are almost certainly associated with weapons of mass destruction. Additionally, coming just one year after the 9/11 attacks, it is understandable that the Bush administration focused heavily on the terrorist network threat. However, given that the 2001 QDR had already postulated the asymmetric threat cyber operations could pose, it was an interesting oversight that potential terrorist use of cyberspace was not mentioned.

2004 National Military Strategy and 2005 National Defense Strategy

In a chronological quirk, the NDS that followed this NSS was issued in 2005, while the NMS was released the year before. It is likely that these documents were drafted in parallel, but the Chairman, Joint Chiefs of Staff released the NMS sooner. The 2004 NMS acknowledged that, "The National Military Strategy is guided by the goals and objectives contained in the President's 'National Security Strategy' and serves to implement the Secretary of Defense's 'National Defense Strategy of the United States of America.'"[46] Of note, the 2005 NDS made the first mention of cyberspace as being part of the "global commons," a term historically used to describe the maritime environment, but later expanded to include the air and space domains as well. Beyond acknowledging

---

[46]Chairman, Joint Chiefs of Staff, *2004 National Military Strategy*, viii.

that the US ability to operate in cyberspace was important, the NDS made a substantive

doctrinal shift by declaring cyberspace "a new theater of operations" and that

"information operations (IO) is becoming a core military competency" which "requires

fundamental shifts in processes, policies, and culture."[47] These bold statements invite

more discussion, but they are the extent to which the NDS addressed cyberspace.

Disappointedly, the NMS added very little to the discussion of developing IO, which

included cyberspace and much more, into a core military competency. The NMS,

however, identified eight capability areas that would "provide a transformation focus for

the Department." "Operating from the Commons: Space, International Waters and

Airspace, and Cyberspace" was one of them.[48] The NMS made one important

contribution to the discussion in its description of the "battle space."

> The non-linear nature of the current security environment requires multi-layered
> active and passive measures to counter numerous diverse conventional and
> asymmetric threats. These include conventional weapons, ballistic and cruise
> missiles and WMD/E. They also include threats in cyberspace aimed at networks
> and data critical to US information-enabled systems. Such threats require a
> comprehensive concept of deterrence encompassing traditional adversaries,
> terrorist networks and rogue states able to employ any range of capabilities.[49]

This paragraph described uniqueness of cyberspace within the non-linear security

environment and it identified not just the threat vector (cyber), but the target (networks

and critical data) along with the need for a multi-layered defense. In emphasizing the

cyber threat, the NMS surmised, "cyber attacks on US commercial information systems

---

[47]Department of Defense, *The National Defense Strategy of the United States of America* (Washington, DC: Government Printing Office, 2005), 16.

[48]Chairman, Joint Chiefs of Staff, *2004 National Military Strategy*, 23.

[49]Ibid., 18.

or attacks against transportation networks may have a greater economic or psychological effect than a relatively small release of a lethal agent."[50]

QDR 2006–NSS 2006–NDS 2008

2006 Quadrennial Defense Review

The 2001 QDR spoke of the potential for technological advances, and addressed cyber attacks as a future possibility. The 2006 QDR acknowledged electronic and cyber as areas that the country might be susceptible to attacks; areas that must be addressed in order to secure the United States in depth.[51] It also addressed cyber capabilities that must be developed and deployed to provide credible deterrence, specifically:

1. Capabilities to shape and defend cyberspace.

2. Joint command and control capabilities that are survivable in the face of WMD, electronic or cyber-attack.

3. Capabilities to locate, tag, and track terrorists in all domains, including cyberspace.[52]

Beyond terrorists and their networks, this QDR named nation-states, such as China, as threats. China in particular might develop and employ such asymmetric capabilities as part of their national strategy.[53] While the QDR acknowledged that DOD must work with interagency partners, such as DHS and federal agencies, to secure cyberspace, it also

---

[50]Ibid., 1.

[51]Department of Defense, *Quadrennial Defense Review Report* (Washington, DC: Government Printing Office, 2006), 24.

[52]Ibid., 23 and 32.

[53]Ibid., 29.

stated that DOD must "Strengthen the coordination of defensive and offensive cyber missions across the Department."[54]

2006 National Security Strategy

Issued just one month after the 2006 QDR, the NSS mentioned cyber just once in 54 pages. Rather than offer something new, the NSS repeated the QDR categorizations when it included cyber in the "Disruptive" challenge category. This category consisted of "challenges from state and non-state actors who employ technologies and capabilities (such as biotechnology, cyber and space operations, or directed-energy weapons) in new ways to counter military advantages the United States currently enjoys."[55]

2008 National Defense Strategy

The final document was the 2008 NDS. This NDS took a similar approach to cyber, as the earlier QDR had. It acknowledged the threats cyber posed to critical infrastructure, and the need for credible deterrence. While DOD has a key supporting role to play in cybersecurity, the NDS concluded that it was not the best overall lead agency for the national effort. China was also specifically cited as "developing technologies to disrupt our traditional examples. Examples include development of anti-satellite capabilities and cyber warfare."[56]

---

[54]Ibid., 51.

[55]White House, *The National Security Strategy of the United States of America* (Washington, DC: Government Printing Office, 2006), 44.

[56]Department of Defense, *2008 National Defense Strategy,* 22.

A Renewed Cyber Focus–The Obama Administration

QDR 2010–NSS 2010–NMS 2011–NDS 2012

Once again, all four types of national strategic documents of the strategic document quartet were issued within a short timeframe. Unlike the quartet of documents presented under the Bush Administration, all four documents here were both drafted and issued well into the Obama Administration's term. Additionally, while termed "NDS 2012," this guidance document was issued under the name *Sustaining U.S. Global Leadership: Priorities for 21st Century Defense.*

2010 Quadrennial Defense Review

The 2010 QDR showed a remarkable expansion in the depth and breadth in DOD's response to the growing relevance of cyber issues. The QDR is peppered with references to cyber and how it will influence future military actions and national defense. For the first time in a QDR, "cyber" was prominent. The QDR lists "Operate effectively in cyberspace" as one of six key mission areas that the DOD "must further rebalance its policy, doctrine and capabilities to better support."[57] Appropriately, the document also included an entire subsection of the same title detailing DOD requirements. Similar to the 2006 QDR, deterrence of US adversaries was a key DOD strategy. Cyber capabilities are a key enabler in a credible deterrence posture.[58] To ensure DOD cyber capabilities meet the warfighter's needs, DOD has laid out the following strategy to grow its cyber organization and policies:

---

[57]Department of Defense, *Quadrennial Defense Review Report* (Washington, DC: Government Printing Office, 2010), 2.

[58]Ibid., v.

1. Develop a more comprehensive approach to DOD operations in cyberspace.

2. Develop greater cyber expertise and awareness.

3. Centralize command of cyber operations.

4. Enhance partnerships with other agencies and governments.[59]

Additionally, DOD has emphasized, "protecting critical DOD infrastructure, including space and cyberspace"; and its need to "improve its ability to attribute WMD, space, and cyberspace attacks in order to hold aggressors responsible and deny them the ability to evade detection in new domains or use proxies."[60] In this respect, the QDR expanded upon past editions by delineating the potential perpetrators of cyber attack more clearly. It also conceded that attackers attempted to infiltrate its networks daily. DOD informally categorized cyber threats as criminal, terrorist, and nation-state; all drove its aforementioned four-point cyber strategy. Moreover, while DOD did not specifically refer to CNA as a desired US capability, it alluded to offensive operations when stating it would conduct "effective operations in cyberspace" if deterrence failed.[61] This was a marked shift in cyber strategy as all strategic documents to this point had focused on defensive measures. Even those describing "enabling operations" for cyber infer that these operations would be defensive in nature.

---

[59]Ibid., x.

[60]Ibid., 14.

[61]Ibid., 15.

2010 National Security Strategy

The latest NSS, released in May 2010, makes up for past neglect of cyber issues and follows the QDR's lead in expanding the US treatment of cyber security. It includes a subsection entitled "Secure Cyberspace."[62] Just as the QDR listed cyber as one of its six key mission areas, the NSS listed the development of a strategy to meet the "challenges to the cyber networks we depend upon." as one of the US' top national security priorities.[63]

2011 National Military Strategy

After a seven-year interval, the Joint Chiefs of Staff issued the current NMS in 2011. As expected, it builds on the 2010 QDR and NSS. In particular, it reinforces the notion that cyberspace is a warfighting domain akin to air, land, sea, and space.[64] It also reiterates that from a DOD perspective, Strategic Command and Cyber Command have the lead coordination with interagency partners such as DHS, and with other outside entities. Of special note, when characterizing the risk posed by cyber threats, unlike the previous QDR and NSS, the 2011 NMS avoided attributing any hostile action or intent to nation states. Instead, while the threat is characterized as serious, there is no named adversary.

---

[62]White House, *2010 National Security Strategy*, 27.

[63]Ibid., 4.

[64]Chairman, Joint Chiefs of Staff, *2011National Military Strategy*, 9.

2012 National Defense Strategy

The NDS is the final national strategic document, but the latest version was not issued under that name. In January 2012, the President and Secretary of Defense released a new strategy for DOD entitled *Sustaining U.S. Global Leadership: Priorities for 21st Century Defense*. Like the earlier NMS, this document followed the QDR and NSS lead on cyber. Unlike past documents, this guidance used the same language contained in previous strategies, demonstrating no conceptual advancement or any new strategy regarding cyber issues.

Other Strategic Documents

In addition to the QDR, NSS, NDS, and NMS, several other national strategic policy documents exist. They are stand-alone documents with no updates expected in the near future. A comprehensive listing of strategy documents discovered during the research can be found in Appendix A (see table 13). Among the noteworthy documents are the: *National Strategy for Trusted Identities in Cyberspace*, *National Military Strategy for Cyberspace Operations* (NMS-CO), *National Strategy to Secure Cyberspace*, and *National Strategy for Physical Protection of Critical Infrastructure and Key Assets*.

NMS-CO and NSSC

2006 National Military Strategy for Cyberspace Operations

The classified NMS-CO was published in December 2006, but it has been partially declassified since its publication. A large portion of the document was redacted indicating that the Pentagon, while displaying a degree of openness about its strategy to secure cyberspace, will not reveal its complete strategy any time soon. Table 4 reveals

how the USG defined the legal authorities to conduct cyber operations and the associated

division of labor with respect to US Code authorities and areas of responsibility.

Table 4.		Organizational Cyber Roles and US Code Authority		
US Code	Title	Key Focus	Principal Organization	Role in Cyberspace
Title 6	*Domestic Security*	Homeland Security	Department of Homeland Security	Security of US Cyberspace
Title 10	*Armed Forces*	National Defense	Department of Defense	Secure US Interests by Conducting Military Operations in Cyberspace
Title 18	*Crimes and Criminal Procedure*	Law Enforcement	Department of Justice	Crime Prevention, Apprehension, and Prosecution of Cyberspace Criminals
Title 32	*National Guard*	First Line Defense of the United States	Army National Guard, Air National Guard	Support Defense of US Interests in Cyberspace Through Critical Infrastructure Protection, Domestic Consequence Management and Other Homeland Defense-Related Activities
Title 40	*Public Buildings, Property, and Works*	Chief Information Officer Roles and Responsibilities	All Federal Departments and Agencies	Establish and Enforce Standards for Acquisition and Security of Information Technologies
Title 50	*War and National Defense*	Foreign Intelligence and Counter-Intelligence Activities	Intelligence Community Agencies Aligned Under the Office of the Director of National Intelligence (DNI)	Intelligence Gathering Through Cyberspace on Foreign Intentions, Operations, and Capabilities

Source: Chairman, Joint Chiefs of Staff, *The National Military Strategy for Cyberspace Operations* (Washington, DC: Government Printing Office, 2006), A-1.

The list of strategic guidance documents used to inform this focused NMS is also important and telling in that two reference documents on the page were obscured so the titles and year of issue were unavailable (see table 14). Despite the effort at strategic communications on cybersecurity, there are additional directives and strategies that the USG is unwilling to disclose. It is also important to note that Homeland Security Presidential Directives 5 and 7 as well as the *National Strategy for Homeland Security* are also referenced. This demonstrates two points. First, it reinforces the idea previously addressed within the NSS, NDS and NMS that DOD cannot be a single-source solution for national cybersecurity. Second, interagency cooperation is taking place, or at the very least, DOD is acknowledging HSPDs and using them to determine how it must support the US-wide cybersecurity mission.

The NMS-CO is a complex document that weaves strategy, structure, ways, and priorities into an attempt to arrive at a coherent military cyber policy. The NMS-CO consists of five elements: Strategic Context, Threats and Vulnerabilities, Strategic Considerations, Military Strategic Framework, and Implementation and Assessment.[65] In order to satisfy the military strategic goal of superiority in cyberspace, the NMS-CO outlines five fundamental and six enabling ways to achieve that objective. The fundamental ways include IO, Network Operations, Kinetic Actions, Law Enforcement and Counterintelligence, and Themes and Messages. Enabling ways consist of Science and Technology, Partnering, Intelligence Data and Support to Operations, Situational

---

[65]Chairman, Joint Chiefs of Staff, *The National Military Strategy for Cyberspace Operations* (Washington, DC: Government Printing Office, 2006), 1.

Awareness, Law and Policy, and People.[66] Oddly, it is not until the NMS-CO's final chapter that Strategic Priorities are identified. These include:

1. Gain and maintain the initiative to operate within adversary decision cycles

2. Integrate capabilities across the full range of military operations using cyberspace

3. Build capacity for cyberspace operations

4. Manage risk to cyberspace operations.67

Furthermore, it is not until enclosure C that the NMS-CO addresses the nature of the cyberspace threat. Enclosure C provides six cyber threat categories: Traditional, Irregular, Catastrophic, Disruptive, Natural, and Accidental. This enclosure also characterizes threat actors into six categories. This data was redacted, so no cross comparison of threat types and actors can be conducted. It is interesting that DOD chose to redact the categories it uses for threat types and actors. One would expect that basic classifications or categories would be readily available. This would seem to indicate that DOD is choosing to define cyber threats with a higher degree of fidelity than other federal departments or agencies are doing. Additionally, since this data remains classified, it is likely that DOD's categories of threat actors differ markedly from the FBI's. The FBI uses (1) Organized Crime; (2) State-sponsored; and (3) Terrorist Groups to categorize threats, but its mission is different from DOD so it is natural to have

---

[66]Ibid., ix.

[67]Ibid., 19-20.

different threat categories.[68] A comparison of DOD, DHS, and FBI categorization of the cyber threat is located in Appendix A (see table 15).

The National Strategy to Secure Cyberspace

The National Strategy to Secure Cyberspace (NSSC) is the most ambitious strategic document dealing with cyber. Published in 2003, it represented the USG's best attempt to define the cyber security problem and to provide a comprehensive solution. Whereas other strategic documents barely touched upon the issue of cybersecurity, acknowledging its importance only as an enabler to accomplish another task, the NSSC identified priorities of action, and it addressed certain technical solutions. The NSSC is specific about which agency or organization is tasked with which responsibility and where government shortfalls occur. Additionally, it provided the U.S. government with recommended actions to strengthen national cybersecurity. These are tied to the NSSC's five priorities of action. Unique among all the national strategic documents reviewed, the NSSC resulted from collaboration between the executive branch, state and local governments, industry, academia and the public. President Bush highlighted the need for continued cooperation between the public and private sector. While the NSSC is focused primarily on government actions within the cybersecurity arena, a public-private partnership is emphasized. "The purpose of this document is to engage and empower Americans to secure the portions of cyberspace that they own, operate, control, or with

---

[68]Federal Bureau of Investigation, "The Cyber Threat: Part I: On the Front Lines with Shawn Henry," http://www.fbi.gov/news/stories/2012/march/shawn-henry032712 (accessed November 7, 2012).

which they interact."[69] From these simple statements of purpose, the objectives, critical

priorities, major actions and initiatives, and actions and recommendations rapidly branch

out in a complex web of priorities and tasking (see table 5). Table 4 simplifies the ever-

widening web of ideas found in the NSSC.

Table 5. National Strategy to Secure Cyberspace			
Purpose	**Strategic Objectives**	**Critical Priorities for Cyberspace Security**	**Actions and Initiatives**
Engage and empower Americans to secure the portions of cyberspace that they own, operate, control, or with which they interact	Prevent cyber attacks against America's critical infrastructures	I. A National Cyberspace Security Response System	1. Establish a public-private architecture for responding to national-level cyber incidents
			2. Provide for the development of tactical and strategic analysis of cyber attacks and vulnerability assessment
			3. Encourage the development of a private sector capability to share a synoptic view of the health of cyberspace
			4. Expand the Cyber Warning and Information Network to support the role of DHS in coordinating crisis management for cyberspace security
			5. Improve national incident management
			6. Coordinate processes for voluntary participation in the development of national public-private continuity and contingency plans
			7. Exercise cybersecurity continuity plans for federal systems
			8. Improve and enhance public-private information sharing involving cyber attacks, threats, and vulnerabilities
	Reduce national vulnerability to cyber attacks	II. A National Cyberspace Security Threat and Vulnerability Reduction Program	1. Enhance law enforcement's capabilities for preventing and prosecuting cyberspace attacks
			2. Create a process for national vulnerability assessments to better

---

[69]White House, *The National Strategy to Secure Cyberspace* (Washington, DC: Government Printing Office, 2003), iii, vii, x-xiii.

49

			understand the potential consequences of threats and vulnerabilities
			3. Secure the mechanisms of the Internet by improving protocols and routing
			4. Foster the use of trusted digital control systems/supervisory control and data acquisition systems
			5. Reduce and remediate software vulnerabilities
			6. Understand infrastructure interdependencies and improve the physical security of cyber systems and telecommunications
			7. Prioritize federal cybersecurity research and development agendas
			8. Assess and secure emerging systems
	Minimize damage and recovery time from cyber attacks that do occur	III. A National Cyberspace Security Awareness and Training Program	1. Promote a comprehensive national awareness program to empower all Americans-businesses, the general workforce, and the general population-to secure their own parts of cyberspace
			2. Foster adequate training and education programs to support the Nation's cybersecurity needs
			3. Increase the efficiency of existing federal cybersecurity training programs
			4. Promote private-sector support for well-coordinated, widely recognized professional cybersecurity certifications
		IV. Securing Governments' Cyberspace	1. Continuously assess threats and vulnerabilities to federal cyber systems
			2. Authenticate and maintain authorized users of federal cyber systems
			3. Secure federal wireless local area networks
			4. Improve security in government outsourcing and procurement
			5. Encourage state and local governments to consider establishing information technology security programs and participate in information sharing and analysis centers with similar governments
		V. National Security and International Cyberspace Security Cooperation	1. Strengthen cyber-related counterintelligence efforts
			2. Improve capabilities for attack attribution and response
			3. Improve coordination for responding to cyber attacks within the U.S. national security community

			4. Work with industry and through international organizations to facilitate dialogue and partnerships among international public and private sectors focused on protecting information infrastructures and promoting a global "culture of security"
			5. Foster the establishment of national and international watch-and-warning networks to detect and prevent cyber attacks as they emerge
			6. Encourage other nations to accede to the Council of Europe Convention on Cybercrime, or to ensure that their laws and procedures are at least as comprehensive.

Source: White House, *The National Strategy to Secure Cyberspace* (Washington, DC: Government Printing Office, 2003), x-xiii.

Other Plans and Policy Documents

In addition to stand-alone national strategy documents, several documents also serve to guide future policy. Some are reviews of existing policies used to identify strengths and shortcomings, such as the *Cyberspace Policy Review*, while others, like the *Comprehensive National Cybersecurity Initiative*, seek to have wide reaching impact on the cybersecurity landscape.

2009 Cyberspace Policy Review

President Obama ordered a 60-day review of USG cybersecurity policy and organization at the beginning of his administration. *Cyberspace Policy Review: Assuring a Trusted and Resilient Information and Communications Infrastructure* appeared in May 2009. It is unique among executive level documents in that it not only presents the challenges of cybersecurity but also lists several shortcomings of the USG organization and policy. In fact, the document paints a bleak picture of U.S. cybersecurity,

51

acknowledging upfront "the Nation's digital infrastructure, based largely upon the Internet, is not secure or resilient."[70] The document also reveals that the nation has already suffered several "intrusions" that have cost the country both hundreds of millions of dollars as well as the loss of intellectual property and military secrets, while other attacks have risked damaging critical infrastructure.[71] As shocking as the toll of poor cybersecurity is made out to be, the review makes the bold and almost fatalistic statement that "The Federal government is not organized to address this growing problem [cybersecurity] effectively now or in the future."[72] While pessimistic, the review did address corrective measures the USG must take.

The review first identified a key shortcoming within the USG cybersecurity organizational structure. "Responsibilities for cybersecurity are distributed across a wide array of federal departments and agencies, many with overlapping authorities, and none with sufficient decision authority to direct actions that deal with often conflicting authorities, and none with sufficient decision authority to direct actions that deal with often conflicting issues in a consistent way."[73] In order to help rectify USG shortcomings, the documents identified ten items as a near term action plan, along with fourteen items that made up a mid-term plan. Both plans are included in their entirety in Annex A (see tables 16 and 17).

---

[70]White House, *Cyberspace Policy Review* (Washington, DC: Government Printing Office, 2009), i.

[71]Ibid.

[72]Ibid.

[73]Ibid.

The top near-term action within President Obama's Cyberspace Policy Review was to "Appoint a cybersecurity policy official responsible for coordinating the Nation's cybersecurity policies and activities. The Obama administration has appointed a Cybersecurity Coordinator (a.ka.Cyber Czar), and created a Cybersecurity Office within the National Security Staff. Aside from having regular access to the President and working closely with the Federal Chief Information Officer, Federal Chief Technology Officer and the National Economic Council, it is unclear what authorities and responsibilities the position holds.[74]

Comprehensive National Cybersecurity Initiative (CNCI)

The *Comprehensive National Cybersecurity Initiative* was released in 2010 as an unclassified outline of the CNCI program started under the Bush administration. It contains three goals and twelve initiatives designed to increase cybersecurity (see table 6).

---

[74]White House, "National Security Council: Cybersecurity," http://www.whitehouse.gov/cybersecurity (accessed November 14, 2012).

Table 6. NCI Goals and Initiatives		
Goal #1: To establish a front line of defense against today's immediate threats by creating or enhancing shared situational awareness of network vulnerabilities, threats, and events within the Federal Government- and ultimately with state, local, and tribal governments and private sector partners-and the ability to act quickly to reduce our current vulnerabilities and prevent intrusions.	**Goal #2: To defend against the full spectrum of threats** by enhancing U.S. counterintelligence capabilities and increasing the security of the supply chain for key information technologies.	**Goal #3: To strengthen the future cybersecurity environment** by expanding cyber education; coordinating and redirecting research and development efforts across the Federal Government; and working to define and develop strategies to deter hostile or malicious activity in cyberspace.
Initiative #1: Manage the Federal Enterprise Network as a single network enterprise with Trusted Internet Connections.		
Initiative #2: Deploy an intrusion detection system of sensors across the Federal enterprise		
Initiative #3: Pursue deployment of intrusion prevention systems across the Federal enterprise		
Initiative #4: Coordinate and redirect research and development (R&D) efforts		
Initiative #5: Connect current cyber ops centers to enhance situational awareness		
Initiative #6: Develop and implement a government-wide cyber counterintelligence (CI) plan		
Initiative #7: Increase the security of our classified networks		
Initiative #8: Expand cyber education		
Initiative #9: Define and develop enduring "leap-ahead" technology, strategies, and programs		
Initiative #10: Define and develop enduring deterrence strategies and programs		
Initiative #11: Develop a multi-pronged approach for global supply chain risk management		
Initiative #12: Define the Federal role for extending cybersecurity into critical infrastructure domains		

Source: White House, *The Comprehensive National Cybersecurity Initiative* (Washington, DC: Government Printing Office, 2010), 1-5.

Of these, the "Expand Cyber Education" initiative stands out because it is reminiscent of the NPISP's urgent call for trained computer science and information technology specialists.[75] The CNCI stated that there were not enough cybersecurity experts available in either the public or private sector to implement the CNCI effectively, nor did an established federal cybersecurity career field yet exist. The CNCI also

---

[75]White House, *National Plan for Information Systems Protection*, v.

highlighted the lack of unity of effort in developing trained cybersecurity personnel.[76]

These two points are especially troubling because the NPISP was released ten years prior to Obama's CNCI.

United States Cyber Organization

The US cyber organization is extremely complex. The most efficient way to understand the organization is to deconstruct it. There are three primary entities, one secondary area, and other tertiary components. Primary areas of cyber responsibility for the USG reside within the DOD, DHS, and DOJ. A significant, but secondary component is composed of the six national cybersecurity centers. These include the United States Computer Emergency Readiness Team (US-CERT), United States Cyber Command (USCYBERCOM), National Cyber Investigative Joint Task Force (NCIJTF), National Security Agency/Central Security Service Threat Operations Center (NTOC), Defense Cyber Crime Center (DC3) and the Intelligence Community–Incident Response Center (IC-IRC). Tertiary components of the cyber organization consist of other government agencies and entities that play a supporting role. Additionally, while some strategic documents point to the role that private industry, state and local governments, and academia must play in implementing cybersecurity, in keeping with scope of the primary research topic, discussion is limited to the federal agencies and federal entities.

---

[76]White House, *The Comprehensive National Cybersecurity Initiative* (Washington, DC: Government Printing Office, 2010), 8.

55

Department of Defense

DOD cyber organization is outlined in figure 1. Of special note, the Director of the National Security Agency is dual-hatted as the Commander, U.S. Cyber Command, which is a subordinate unified command under U.S. Strategic Command. Additionally, because of the first *DOD Cyber Operations Plan* in May 2012, regional Combatant Commanders established the depicted Joint Cyber Centers. These centers used in-house cyber personnel. The Combat Support Elements shown are co-located with the combatant commands, but their personnel belong to U.S. Cyber Command. The purpose of the Joint Cyber Centers is to act as the 'nexus for combatant command cyberspace enterprise' as well as directing the offensive and defensive cyber operations at the commands. [77] The Combat Support Elements assist the Joint Cyber Centers and act as on-site liaisons for U.S. Cyber Command. The DOD Cyber Operations Plan is not available, however, the creation of the Joint Cyber Centers and Combat Support Elements were widely reported via defense and technology focused news agencies in June 2012. [78] The DOD structure contained three of the six national cybersecurity centers listed within the Comprehensive National Cybersecurity Initiative. These included NSA's Threat Operations Center, DOD's Cyber Crime Center (operated by the Department of the Air Force), and USCYBERCOM (which absorbed the role previously carried out by Joint Task Force–

---

[77]Zachary Fryer-Biggs, "Panetta Green Lights First Cyber Operations Plan," Defensenews.com, http://www.defensenews.com/article/20120606/DEFREG02/ 306060010/Panetta-Green-Lights-First-Cyber-Operations-Plan (accessed November 7, 2012).

[78]Ibid.

Global Network Operations). The latter organization was disestablished upon

USCYBERCOM's creation.[79]

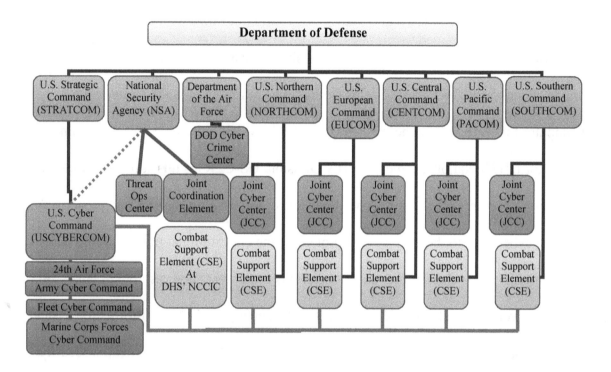

Figure 1.   Department of Defense Cyber Organization

Source: Created by author.

Department of Homeland Security

DHS Cyber Organization is outlined in figure 2. Of particular interest are the

existence of two 24/7 watch-centers dedicated to ensuring the nation's cybersecurity

health and safety. First, there is the National Cybersecurity and Communications

[79]Secretary, Department of Defense, *Memorandum: Establishment of a Subordinate Unified U.S. Cyber Command Under U.S. Strategic Command for Military Cyberspace Operations* (Washington, DC: Government Printing Office, 2009).

Integration Center (NCCIC). The NCCIC functions as a 24/7 fusion center. It is responsible for the "common operating picture for cyber and communications across federal, state, and local government, intelligence and law enforcement communities and the private sector."[80] In the event of a cyber or communications incident, NCCIC acts as the national response center, coordinating the federal response in conjunction with state and local authorities and private sector entities. The other center is the United States Computer Emergency Readiness Team (US-CERT) which acts as the 24/7 operations center for DHS's National Cyber Security Division. US-CERT's mission is to "improve the nation's cybersecurity posture, coordinate cyber information sharing, and proactively manage cyber risks to the nation while protecting the constitutional rights of Americans." It accomplishes this charter through its operations center that "accepts, triages, and collaboratively responds to incidents; provides technical assistance to information system operators; and disseminates timely notifications regarding current and potential security threats and vulnerabilities."[81] US-CERT is also one of the six national cybersecurity centers outlined within the Comprehensive National Cybersecurity Initiative.

---

[80]Department of Homeland Security, "About the National Cybersecurity and Communications Integration Center (NCCIC)," http://www.dhs.gov/about-national-cybersecurity-communications-integration-center-nccic (accessed November 10, 2012).

[81]Department of Homeland Security United States Computer Emergency Readiness Team (US-CERT), "About the Department of Homeland Security's United States Computer Emergency Readiness Team (US-CERT)," http://www.us-cert.gov/about-us (accessed November 10, 2012).

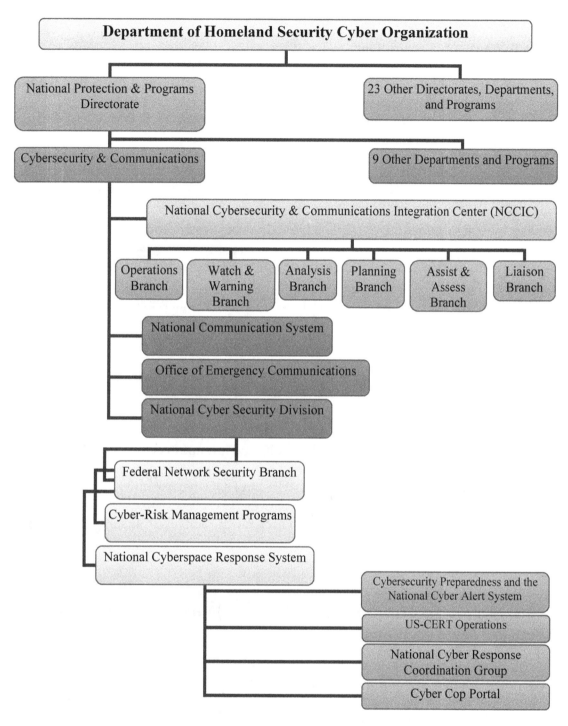

Figure 2.   Department of Homeland Security Cyber Organization

Source: Created by author.

Department of Justice

Federal Bureau of Investigation

As the lead for criminal investigations within the Department of Justice, the FBI

has purview over law enforcement matters related to cybercrime, to include criminals,

foreign adversaries, and terrorists.[82] "Protect the United States against cyber-based

attacks and high-technology crimes" is number three among the FBI's top ten priorities.[83]

To accomplish this mission, the FBI has its own cyber organization, the Cyber Division,

located within its headquarters element (see figure 3). The Cyber Division accomplishes

the FBI's cyber mission through the National Cyber Investigative Joint Task Force

(NCIJTF) and cyber investigative squads located at each of the Bureau's 56 field

offices.[84] The NCIJTF is the "focal point for all government agencies to coordinate,

integrate, and share information related to all domestic cyber threat investigations."[85] The

NCIJTF has a global mission and consists of IC and law enforcement members. Unlike

the defense-oriented theme embedded in DHS and DOD cybersecurity strategies,

NCIJTF seeks to increase the security of cyberspace by actively "pursuing the terrorists,

---

[82]Federal Bureau of Investigation, *The Cyber Threat: Part I: On the Front Lines with Shawn Henry.*

[83]Federal Bureau of Investigation, "About Us: Quick Facts," http://www.fbi.gov/about-us/quick-facts (accessed November 10, 2012).

[84]Department of Justice, Audit Report 11-22, *The Federal Bureau of Investigation's Ability to Address the National Security Cyber Intrusion Threat* (Washington, DC: Government Printing Office, 2011), ii-iii.

[85]Federal Bureau of Investigation, "About Us: National Cyber Investigative Joint Task Force," http://www.fbi.gov/about-us/investigate/cyber/ncijtf (accessed November 10, 2012).

spies, and criminals who seek to exploit our systems."[86] Of note, the section chief for the FBI's Cyber National Security Section is also the director of the NCIJTF, which is one of the six national cybersecurity centers outlined within the Comprehensive National Cybersecurity Initiative.

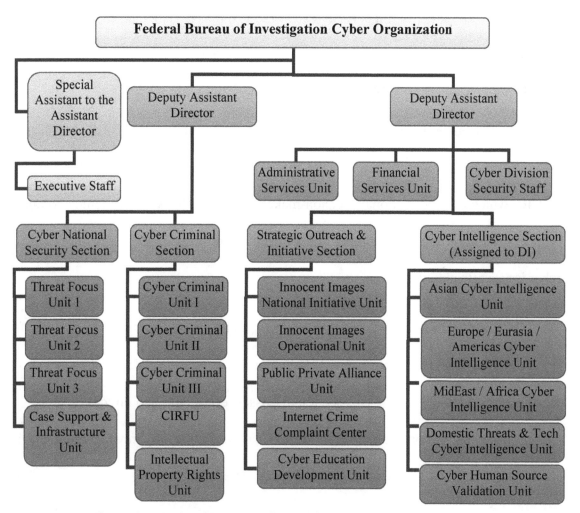

Figure 3.   Federal Bureau of Investigation Cyber Organization

Source: Created by author.

---

[86]Ibid.

National Cybersecurity Centers

The Comprehensive National Cybersecurity Initiative within NSPD-54/HSPD-23 created six cybersecurity centers located across the USG to tackle the wide spectrum of cybersecurity considerations. These centers have mission sets that range from incident response to training/exercises to research and development. The six centers are: (1) NTOC; (2) US-CERT; (3) USCYBERCOM; (4) DC3; (5) NCIJTF; and (6) IC-IRC. These centers primarily reside within DOD, DHS, and DOJ, each serving to gather specific domain- related (Defense, Civil, Intelligence, and Law Enforcement/Counterintelligence) information relevant to cybersecurity. These centers share information with each other and the NCCIC. The information is fused at the NCCIC, which provides national decision-makers and the USG with a coherent, common cyber operating picture that improves situational awareness and understanding of the cyber issues affecting the nation.

Laws, Directives and Proposed Legislation

The legal landscape governing U.S. cybersecurity is as complex as its organization and policy goals. This section discusses recent laws and directives, along with proposed legislation in an effort to identify the systematic way in which the USG is attempting to deal with growing concerns over cybersecurity.

Homeland Security Act of 2002

The Homeland Security Act of 2002 (HSA) is the primary legislation dealing with cybersecurity. The law's primary effect was to establish the Department of Homeland

Security, but it also empowered the DHS with a multi-faceted mission in which three of its seven primary directives apply to cybersecurity:

1. Prevent terrorist attacks within the United States.

2. Reduce the vulnerability of the United States to terrorism

3. Carry out all functions of entities transferred to the Department, including by acting as a focal point regarding natural and manmade crises and emergency planning.[87]

None of these objectives included "cyber." That is understandable since the term was just beginning to enter the government's lexicon in 2002. Following the 9/11 attacks, the act's focus was countering terrorism. While the origin and intent of cybersecurity threats may not be terrorism, the mission of cybersecurity is an implied task. By enhancing the security of America's cyber realm, vulnerability to cyber-borne terrorism is reduced and targets reliant on cyberspace such as critical infrastructure can be better protected.

Aside from the Secretary of Homeland Security, the act created three other positions with cybersecurity related duties. These included the Undersecretary for Information Analysis and Infrastructure Protection, Undersecretary for Emergency Preparedness and Response within DHS, and the creation of the Office of Science and Technology within the Department of Justice, led by the Assistant Attorney General, Office of Justice Programs. The former positions, both within DHS, are referenced within

---

[87]United States, *Homeland Security Act of 2002* (Washington, DC: Government Printing Office, 2002), sec 101.

the Act as having duties related to the "Enhancement of Non-Federal Cybersecurity."[88] In essence, these positions provide state and local governments with analysis, indications, and warnings of threats to the critical information systems and technical assistance to the private sector in developing emergency action plans in preparation for loss of critical information systems.[89] Among the many Department of Justice missions, one was to manage the development and acquisition of tools to counter cybercrime at the federal, state and local law enforcement levels.

In addition to establishing DHS, this piece of legislation was embedded with the Cyber Security Enhancement Act of 2002. The title is misleading. This legislation did nothing to enhance cyber security directly. Instead, its primary purpose was deterrence. By amending sentencing guidelines for cyber related crimes, the law directed the US Sentencing Commission to consider the following:

1. Whether the defendant acted with malicious intent to cause harm in committing the offense.

2. Whether the offense involved a computer used by the government in furtherance of national defense, national security, or the administration of justice.

3. Whether the violation was intended to or had the effect of significantly interfering with or disrupting a critical infrastructure.

---

[88]Ibid., sec 223.

[89]Ibid.

4. Whether the violation was intended to or had the effect of creating a threat to public health or safety or injury to any person.[90]

Presidential Directives

Homeland Security Presidential Directive-5

HSPD-5, *Management of Domestic Incidents*, followed the HSA in February 2003. It expanded upon the responsibilities for DHS to manage domestic incidents. This directive designated the Secretary of Homeland Security as "the principal Federal official for domestic incident management."[91] In order to enhance the nation's ability to manage domestic incidents, HSPD-5 directed the DHS Secretary to create and administer a National Incident Management System (NIMS) and National Response Plan (NRP). The NIMS's purpose was to facilitate the ability of "Federal, State, and local governments to work effectively and efficiently together to prepare for, respond to, and recover from domestic incidents, regardless of cause, size, or complexity."[92] The NRP has four overarching purposes:

1. Providing mechanisms for Federal support and direction during incidents.

2. Ensuring cohesion and synergy between Federal emergency management plans.

3. Consistency in incident reporting and analysis mechanisms.

---

[90]Ibid., sec 225.

[91]White House, Homeland Security Presidential Directive (HSPD)-5, *Management of Domestic Incidents* (Washington, DC: Government Printing Office, 2003), 230.

[92]Ibid., 231.

4. Improving incident management through experience, exercises, and

technology.[93]

Homeland Security Presidential Directive-7

HSPD-7, *Critical Infrastructure Identification, Prioritization, and Protection* was

issued in December 2003 and identified issues associated with critical infrastructure,

prioritization and protection. In doing so, it also expanded the DHS mission by stating the

federal government's policy to protect critical infrastructure and key resources against

terrorism and then listing specific effects that must be prevented (see table 7).[94]

Table 7. U.S. Policy for Protection of Critical Infrastructure Against Terrorism.	
It is the policy of the United states to enhance the protection of our Nation's critical infrastructure and key resources against terrorist acts that could:	
1	Cause catastrophic health effects or mass casualties comparable to those from the use of a weapon of mass destruction
2	Impair Federal departments and agencies' abilities to perform essential missions, or to ensure the public's health and safety
3	Undermine State and local government capacities to maintain order and to deliver minimum essential public services
4	Damage the private sector's capability to ensure the orderly functioning of the economy and delivery of essential services
5	Have a negative effect on the economy through the cascading disruption of other critical infrastructure and key resources
6	Undermine the public's morale and confidence in our national economic and political institutions

Source: White House, Homeland Security Presidential Directive-7 (HSPD-7), *Critical Infrastructure Identification, Prioritization, and* Protection (Washington, DC: Government Printing Office, 2003), 2.

---

[93]Ibid., 232.

[94]White House, HSPD-7, *Critical Infrastructure Identification, Prioritization, and Protection*, 2.

Arguably, all of these policy sub-topics influence cyberspace and that effective cybersecurity would be one way to ensuring the successful implementation of this policy. HSPD-7 reiterates the Secretary of Homeland Security's responsibility to coordinate the national effort to implement the policy, but it also identified DHS Secretary responsibilities in cyberspace and thoroughly defined the cybersecurity supported/supporting relationship at the federal level. Specifically, the Secretary was directed to "maintain an organization to serve as a focal point for the security of cyberspace." [95] HSPD-7 also established DHS as the supported federal agency in cybersecurity.

The National Cybersecurity and Communications Integration Center (NCCIC) became the organization envisioned by HSPD-7 to focus national cybersecurity efforts. While HSPD-7 restates one of the many responsibilities of the DHS Secretary, this paragraph is significant for because it outlines the supported/supporting relationship between DHS and all other Federal departments and agencies. Regardless of which department or agency possesses cyber expertise, DHS is clearly the supported department unless prohibited by law. This is important. As the cybersecurity arena develops, the nature of this supporting relationship continues to be discussed today, particularly with respect to whether DHS or DOD should act as the executive agent for national cybersecurity.

HSPD-7 is also significant because it expands upon the concept of using "sector-specific" federal agencies to deal with different infrastructure sectors. PDD-63 outlined the idea of sector-specific lead agencies, but it did not provide a comprehensive list, as

---

[95]Ibid., 3.

did HSPD-7. The roles and responsibilities of other departments, agencies and offices are listed in HSPD-7. These sector-specific agencies include the Department of Agriculture, Health and Human Services, Environmental Protection Agency, Department of Energy, Department of the Treasury, Department of the Interior, and the Department of Defense (see table 8). Among the duties of sector-specific departments and agencies is the responsibility to "facilitate sharing of information about physical and cyber threats, vulnerabilities, incidents, potential protective measures and best practices."[96] Remaining federal departments with responsibilities for critical infrastructure and key resources fall into an "Other Departments, Agencies, and Offices" category.[97]

---

[96]Ibid., 5.

[97]Ibid., 3.

Table 8.	Roles and Responsibilities of Sector-Specific Federal Agencies	
Department of Agriculture	Agriculture, Food (meat, poultry, egg products)	Sector-Specific Agencies shall:
Health and Human Services	Public health, Healthcare, and food (other than meat, poultry, egg products)	-Collaborate with all relevant Federal departments and agencies, State and local governments, and the private sector, including with key persons and entities in their infrastructure sector.
Environmental Protection Agency	Drinking water and Water treatment systems	
Department of Energy	Energy, including the production, refining, storage, and distribution of oil, gas, and electric power except for commercial nuclear power facilities	-Conduct or facilitate vulnerability assessments of the sector.
Department of the Treasury	Banking and finance	-Encourage risk management strategies to protect against and mitigate the effects of attacks against critical infrastructure and key resources.
Department of the Interior	National monuments and icons	
Department of Defense	Defense Industrial Base	

Source: White House, Homeland Security Presidential Directive-7 (HSPD-7), *Critical Infrastructure Identification, Prioritization, and Protection* (Washington, DC: Government Printing Office, 2003), 3.

Within the "other" category, for example, the Department of Commerce has specific cybersecurity requirements. It is responsible to "work with private sector, research, academic, and government organizations to improve technology for cyber systems."[98] Moreover, a Critical Infrastructure Protection Policy Coordinating Committee is tasked to "advise the Homeland Security Council on interagency policy related to physical and cyber infrastructure protection."[99] Since HSPD-7 is over nine years old, it might be prudent to update the document to address changes that have occurred in technology or USG policy. A potential change could be that non sector-

[98]Ibid., 4.

[99]Ibid.

specific departments and agencies receive specific cybersecurity related tasking. In this way, a redefined HSPD-7 could expand cybersecurity efforts across more of the USG in response to the growing cybersecurity needs.

Proposed Legislation

The Obama administration has made cybersecurity a priority for the nation and has supported Congress' efforts to pass comprehensive cybersecurity legislation. Congress has recently considered several pieces of legislation that sought to mandate cybersecurity, however, none received enough support to become law. The Obama administration's vision for national cybersecurity is in stark contrast to the opinions of the Clinton and Bush administrations. Both presidents believed that government could not mandate cybersecurity and that a sustainable solution for cybersecurity could only be achieved through partnership between government and the private sector.

Recently considered bills included the *Cyber Intelligence Sharing and Protection Act (CISPA)*, *Strengthening and Enhancing Cybersecurity by Using Research, Education, Information, and Technology Act of 2012 (SECURE IT)*, and the *Cybersecurity Act of 2012*. The Obama administration strongly supported the latter bill.

These bills defined the threat and necessary government actions separately. The Heritage Foundation published a brief factsheet and analysis on the proposed legislation. Key policies and Heritage Foundation analyses are listed below. Analysis from this research project is provided for comparison, when applicable (see table 9).

Each of these proposed bills was defeated, including the *Cybersecurity Act of 2012* that Obama supported. Their supporters, however, hope to gather support for reconsideration. In lieu of a national cybersecurity law, the Obama Administration is currently considering an Executive Order to mandate national cybersecurity requirements. It has been reported that a draft order takes strong cues from the *Cybersecurity Act of 2012.*[100]

---

[100]Morgan Little, "Executive order on cyber security builds steam amid criticisms," *Los Angeles Times*, http://www.latimes.com/news/politics/la-pn-obama-

Cybersecurity Organization, the Intelligence Community and the 9/11 Commission Report

This section provides a comparative analysis between the current cyber organization and the IC deficiencies identified following the 9/11 terrorist attacks. This comparison relies primarily on *The 9/11 Commission Report: Final Report of the National Commission on Terrorist Attacks Upon the United States* to establish a baseline for discussion on IC shortcomings and recommendations offered by the 9/11 Commission to correct them. By identifying the strengths and weaknesses between the stated aims of national policy and existing cybersecurity organizations, this comparison determines if their organizations and policies are more similar to the pre-9/11 or post 9/11 IC.

US cyber policy and organization is complex. Cybersecurity responsibility is integrated across different departments and agencies similar to the IC. The goal of this analysis is to judge whether current cyber policy and organization has adopted the IC lessons learned in the aftermath of 9/11. If US cyber policy and organization is positioned to avoid the pitfalls identified within the pre-9/11 IC, then one could argue that it is postured for the post-9/11 security environment. If not, then US policy and organization could be repeating mistakes of the past, leaving the country more susceptible to a devastating cyber attack.

Rather than undertaking an exhaustive review of the IC, this section avoids revisiting the contentious 9/11 intelligence "failures." The 9/11 Commission recommendations determine which ones are applicable to the current cyber organization.

---

executive-order-cyber-security-20121002,0,6786970.story (accessed November 19, 2012).

This study does not address which recommendations were implemented, nor does it discuss the success or failure of recommendations that were accepted.

The commission's recommendations remain relevant to the cybersecurity discussion because the concepts can be applied to the US cyber organization. The degree of application depends on whether current cyber organization and policies are more similar to the pre or the post-9/11 intelligence community.

The Five Recommendations of the 9/11 Commission

The 9/11 Commission Report made five recommendations. Recommendation #4 suggested restructuring Congressional oversight of the IC. There is no correlation with this recommendation to the existing cybersecurity organizations. As a result, this recommendation is not applicable. The five 9/11 Commission recommendations were:

1. Unifying strategic intelligence and operational planning against Islamic terrorists across the foreign-domestic divide with a National Counterterrorism Center.

2. Unifying the intelligence community with a new National Intelligence Director.

3. Unifying the many participants in the counterterrorism effort and their knowledge in a network-based information-sharing system that transcends traditional governmental boundaries.

4. Unifying and strengthening congressional oversight to improve quality and accountability.

5. Strengthening the FBI and homeland defenders.[101]

---

[101]National Commission on Terrorist Attacks Upon the United States (9/11 Commission), *The 9/11 Commission Report: Final Report of the National Commission*

Recommendation #1: Unity of Effort Across the Foreign-Domestic Divide

This recommendation speaks to leadership and the identification and empowerment of a designated entity to lead national intelligence efforts. The Commission encountered numerous examples that demonstrated the existence of relevant pieces of data across the national security enterprise, but no individual entity had the authority to collate the intelligence, direct action, monitor progress, or resolve interagency conflict. In sum, "Responsibility and accountability were diffuse."[102] In contrast to the IC, as the federal government's recognition of the need to protect critical national infrastructure grew, so too did the realization that a lead agency or entity was needed achieve unity of effort.

This led to the creation of the National Infrastructure Protection Center in 1998. Initially, a non-aligned entity, the FBI housed the center until DHS was created in 2003. The center was renamed the National Infrastructure Coordinating Center and moved to DHS, falling under the department's control. Several NSS's emphasized cybersecurity as essential to protecting infrastructure. It was logical that the NIPC and later NICC also became the government's focal point for cybersecurity indications, warnings, and incident response. This changed in 2008 when DHS established the National Cyber Security Center (NCSC). This organization was short-lived. It became the National Cybersecurity and Communications Information Center (NCCIC) less than 18 months later. The NCCIC maintains the federal government's cyber and communications

---

on Terrorist Attacks Upon the United States (Washington, DC: Government Printing Office, 2004), 400.

[102]Ibid.

common operating picture. It also coordinates among federal, state, local departments and agencies, as well as industry and academia regarding cybersecurity.

Cybersecurity Organization and Recommendation #1: Assessment

From an organizational standpoint, the NCCIC provides the necessary unity of effort for national cybersecurity efforts. The only potential cause for concern is the apparent separation of cybersecurity and communications in the NCCIC from the remaining critical infrastructure the NICC handles. The national security documents reviewed earlier included cyberspace as part of the nation's critical infrastructure because it was *the* connective tissue for all information systems. By separating cybersecurity from the rest of the nation's critical infrastructure, the government introduced yet another organization as a center of excellence. Such a move could inhibit collaboration and hinder information sharing. In this instance, however, the move appears prudent. Cyberspace is a part of America's critical infrastructure and the security of that domain is vital to the nation's interests.

However, cyberspace has also matured in the 17 years since the Clinton administration first emphasized the issue. As cyber issues become more complex, the government must place greater weight on it if the nation is to be successful in securing its critical networks. In this sense, the NCCIC is a natural progression in the development of a government response that does not unnecessarily dilute resources or reduce awareness and response effectiveness. The division of labor between NCCIC and NICC is of less cause for concern because they are both part of the DHS's National Protection and Programs Directorate. With both 24x7-watch centers operated by the same directorate, one should expect minimal problems with information sharing, collaboration, and operating procedures.

Recommendation #2: Unity of Effort in the Intelligence Community

This recommendation strikes at the heart of the perceived IC shortcomings experienced during and after 9/11. It also called for leadership restructuring. This recommendation led to the creation of the Director of National Intelligence (DNI). To make its case for change, *The 9/11 Report* identified six problems. While not comprehensive, each pointed out systemic issues that reduced the efficiency and effectiveness of the IC without focusing on minutia or perceived intelligence failures. Just as the five overarching 9/11 Commission recommendations could be applied to the cybersecurity organization to measure its ability to cope with the post-9/11 security environment, the sub-recommendations for the IC are also applicable. The six problems are:

1. Structural barriers to performing joint intelligence work.

2. Lack of common standards and practices across the foreign-domestic divide.

3. Divided management of national intelligence capabilities.

4. Weak capacity to set priorities and move resources.

5. Too many jobs.

6. Too complex and secret.[103]

---

[103]Ibid., 408.

IC Problem #1: Structural barriers to performing joint intelligence work

This problem refers to the 9/11 Commission's assessment that "National intelligence is still organized around the collection disciplines of the home agencies, not the joint mission. . . . No one component holds all the information"[104] This assessment is equally true for the US cyber organization. With its mission spread out among three different federal departments (Homeland Security, Defense, Justice), each with its own focus (Domestic security, National defense, Law enforcement), no single portion of the US cyber organization has a complete awareness of the entire US cyber picture.

IC Problem #1: Assessment

The US cyber organization suffers from the same problem. DHS is by law and presidential directive the lead for cybersecurity. "The Secretary [DHS] will continue to maintain an organization to serve as a focal point for the security of cyberspace. The organization will facilitate interactions and collaborations between and among Federal departments and agencies, State and local governments, the private sector, academia and international organizations."[105] Despite this clear designation of the DHS Secretary as the "supported" leader for U.S. cybersecurity efforts, the Homeland Security Act of 2002 and HSPD-7 did not grant the Secretary control of all U.S. cybersecurity efforts. DHS would be "supported" by the rest of the federal government, or at best, it was responsible for unity of effort. "To the extent permitted by law, Federal departments and agencies with cyber expertise, including but not limited to the Departments of Justice, Commerce, the

---

[104]Ibid.

[105]White House, HSPD-7, 3.

Treasury, Defense, Energy, and State, and the CIA, will collaborate with and support the organization in accomplishing its mission."[106]

While attempting to establish a clear supported and supporting relationship, the *Homeland Security Act* and HSPD-7 end up creating a system similar to the joint military arena, a system where the other services support a Joint Force Commander that has no statutory operational control of the supporting organizations. To illustrate, a Joint Force Commander does not need to control an entire service to receive the specialized support that a specific service can provide. Normally, the Joint Task Force is contained within or defined by a specific geographic area. Cyberspace, however, is a distinct operational environment, one that is not constrained by the traditional limits of the physical world. Actions within cyberspace can potentially reach any location worldwide nearly instantaneously.

Only three other joint organizations have had a worldwide mission. Each was subordinate to the DOD's United States Strategic Command (USSTRATCOM). The first mission was nuclear deterrence, exemplified by the old strategic triad (ICBM, SSBN, and Strategic Bombers). The second, Joint Task Force-Global Network Operations (JTF-GNO) was responsible for the DOD's defensive CNO. The third, Joint Functional Component Command–Network Warfare (JFCC-NW) was responsible for DOD's offensive CNO. The latter two organizations were disestablished in 2010 when USCYBERCOM was created. USCYBERCOM, however, is a sub-unified command

---

[106]Ibid.

subordinate to USSTRATCOM. USCYBERCOM is a joint command manned by members of all services. It also leads commands service cyber organizations.[107]

HSA and HSPD-7 seek a "joint" solution to the problem of cybersecurity organization. This is an inadequate solution given the size of the U.S. cybersecurity organization. Control and direction must reside at a higher echelon. If the "joint" model enshrined in the HSA or HSPD-7 is followed, DOD would be a better choice for the supported commander role. The bulk of the US cyber organization's intellectual strength and expertise lies within the DOD's cyber arm. DOD draws its joint strength through its service components, while the DHS, and to a lesser degree the DOJ, lacks diverse in-house cyber components and must rely on assistance from external organizations. In sum, the 9/11 Commission remains applicable to the U.S. cybersecurity organization, despite the goals and intent of the HSA and HSPD-7.

IC problem #2: Lack of common standards and
practices across the foreign-domestic divide

In stating the problem, the 9/11 Commission called for intelligence work to have a "common standard of quality in how it is collected, processed (e.g., translated), reported, shared, and analyzed."[108] The Commission remarked, "A common set of personnel standards for intelligence can create a group of professionals better able to operate in

---

[107]United States Strategic Command, "U.S. Strategic Command History," http://www.stratcom.mil/history (accessed November 10, 2012); United States Strategic Command, "U.S. Cyber Command," http://www.stratcom.mil/factsheets/cyber_command (accessed November 10, 2012).

[108]9/11 Commission, *9/11 Report*, 409.

joint activities, transcending their own service-specific mindsets."[109] In calling for individual agencies to transcend parochial interests, the 9/11 Commission echoed the previous problem, and recommended that the IC act in a manner similar to the joint structure the Goldwater-Nichols Act of 1986 created.[110]

IC Problem #2: Assessment

This assessment has two sub-problems. The first is directed at the entire IC where different departments and agencies have developed distinctive standards. There are many challenges associated with a singular reporting mechanism. One of these challenges is the particular vehicles used for reporting information and finished intelligence. These differences could be technical (hardware or software) or administrative in nature. For example, each department and agency is responsible for acquiring the hardware and software that best suit its mission. Changing technical reasons often involve systems or programs that are costly to procure and manage. The administration of how a final product is displayed or reported can be relatively easy to adjust, but if it is directly linked to unique software or systems, then it can also be difficult to change. To standardize reporting involves changing how leaders manage budgets as well as the acquisition and procurement process. Leadership and resource management are discussed later.

The second sub-problem is personnel management. The 9/11 commission argued that unified personnel standards within the IC would enhance joint interoperability and

---

[109]Ibid.

[110]United States, "Goldwater Nichols Department of Defense Reorganization Act of 1986," National Defense University Library, http://www.ndu.edu/library/goldnich/ goldnich.html#97 (accessed November 14, 2012).

effectiveness. While this may be true, the IC consists of 15 different departments and agencies. Each has developed its own personnel standards. While Congress could mandate change, it has chosen not to do so. Given the momentum for change post-9/11, it is unclear why Congress did not act upon this 9/11 Commission recommendation. A potential explanation is that personnel standards are embedded within individual departments and agencies. Not all IC members are wholly dedicated to intelligence, the FBI and Department of Energy, for example, have other responsibilities. It would be difficult to align the intelligence components of IC members without having unintended consequences on the remainder of their personnel structures.

While this problem-set is applicable to the cybersecurity apparatus, it has pitfalls. Because the joint environment exists within a singular Department (DOD), it is not as easy to apply to the entire cyber organization. Each cyber organization has a different culture. Different personnel standards evolved from unique mission sets and requirements. Mandating change to overcome these cultural differences would be difficult. The Goldwater-Nichols Act of 1986 is especially illustrative. One of the key means to enforce service compliance was that officers with the rank of Colonel or Captain (O-6) needed to be "Joint Qualified" in order to be eligible for promotion to the rank of General or Admiral (O-7). The Joint Specialty Officer qualification is comprised of three distinct parts (Joint Professional Military Education Phase I, three years in a designated Joint assignment, and Joint Professional Military Education Phase II). While the Goldwater-Nichols Act did not prohibit the services from using joint qualifications as a promotion discriminator for ranks below O-7, the Act ensured that it was a prerequisite for O-7. Interpreted another way, the services can ignore joint qualification for the

82

majority of its personnel. This decreases the population which could be expected to be "professionals better able to operate in joint activities, transcending their own service-specific mindsets." as desired by the 9/11 Commission.[111]

The Joint Specialty Officer model is a useful example, but it would be challenging to establish a personnel system similar to that envisioned by the 9/11 Commission across a loose coalition such as the IC or the cybersecurity organization. There is value in "joint" education and experience, but it is harder to apply a "mandatory" component of it within the cybersecurity organization without unified personnel standards (i.e. rank structure).

IC Problem #3: Divided management of national intelligence capabilities

Just as the 9/11 Commission called for unified reporting and personnel standards and structure, it also highlighted that the IC lacked strong centralized leadership. Friction points existed within the IC where an individual agency's needs and priorities conflicted with other IC members. This conflict was evident in highly technical areas where resources were scarce, but in high demand. The U.S. cybersecurity shares this same type of environment where technical capabilities and skilled cyber personnel are in high-demand but have a low-density.

IC Problem #3: Assessment

Despite the lack of unity of command within the U.S. cybersecurity organization, the evidence suggests that there is little to no friction between departments or agencies. There are no significant interagency issues regarding the distribution of cyber personnel

---

[111]9/11 Commission, *9/11 Report*, 409.

83

either. Issues of divided management may exist. A large-scale cyber attack could reveal weaknesses within the multi-Department cybersecurity organization and its personnel system but the goal is to avoid that type of discovery.

IC Problem #4: Weak capacity to set priorities and move resources

In this item, the 9/11 Commission noted that while members of the IC are organized for specific purposes, they all work to satisfy national intelligence priorities. The Commission suggested that the Director of Central Intelligence (DCI) be empowered to adjust priority of effort across the IC.[112] While the Commission gave no specific examples, it implied that the Director would have not only oversight but direction over IC member activities. This was an unusual concept since the Director's position was equal to some IC members, but inferior in rank to others.

IC Problem #4: Assessment

Unlike the DNI, the Cybersecurity Coordinator position adopted after the *Cyberspace Policy Review* appears to have little authoritative power regarding policy or budget. Without a position equivalent to the DNI, the U.S. cybersecurity organization could suffer from misaligned priorities and sub-optimized assignment of resources among its major departments. While the research found no evidence this has happened, if the cyber organization is supposed to be mutually supportive of its constituent members, an oversight position or entity would be beneficial to ensuring that priorities and resources are aligned across the cyber enterprise.

---

[112]Ibid., 410.

IC Problem #5: Too many jobs

Even with unity of command, the DNI still has a span of control concern. The Commission noted that the DCI has three separate responsibilities. First, he runs the CIA. Second, he has to manage the IC. Lastly, he is the principal intelligence advisor to the President. With such a wide range of duties, the Commission maintained that no one person could manage all three responsibilities effectively. Because of the DCI's span of control concerns and vast responsibilities, the IC suffered. The establishment of the DNI was an attempt to solve this problem.

IC Problem #5: Assessment

Lack of a singular cyber authority similar to the DNI is a clear gap within the U.S. cybersecurity organization. In this respect, today's cybersecurity organization is analogous to the IC prior to 9/11. The DHS Secretary is the nominal head for the cybersecurity organization much as the DCI was for the IC. However, the potential for a leadership failure is exacerbated within DHS because it is such a diverse department. Moreover, cybersecurity is just one aspect of many diverse missions allocated to DHS. The DHS Secretary must also coordinate and collaborate with other departments, agencies, and entities where cybersecurity may also be just one item within a portfolio of missions.

IC Problem #6: Too complex and secret

This represents the most vague of the 9/11 Commission's problems. It decries the IC's complexity and criticizes the IC's secret budget for potentially harming oversight.[113]

---

[113]9/11 Commission, *The 9/11 Commission Report*, 103.

While the report does not criticize the oversight currently exercised by the Senate and House of Representatives, it asserted that those committees lacked the benefit provided to other oversight committees by journalists and watchdog organizations.

IC Problem #6: Assessment

Cybersecurity, whether in the private or public sector, is a technical arena. The proprietary or classified tactics, techniques, further complicate the field. Many aspects of the U.S. cybersecurity organization are secret. This secrecy, whether in terms of organization or budget, is a sound operational security measure but it limits the community's transparency. Given the need for security and secrecy within the IC, the Commission's recommendation to increase oversight by opening the IC's budget to extra-governmental scrutiny could have a detrimental impact to operational security.

Recommendation #3: Unity of Effort in Sharing Information

This recommendation detailed the challenges of sharing information. *The 9/11 Report* acknowledged that while each IC member worked towards the same goal, each organization also shared a culture that erred on the side of compartmentalizing and over classification thereby limiting the sharing of such intelligence. Additionally, each IC member maintained its own stove-piped databases, which were inaccessible by other IC members. In this way, it was difficult for an individual analyst to view information on a topic that might have resided in the IC's myriad of databases. The pitfall here is that it is almost impossible for a single analyst to "connect the dots" of an intelligence problem without access to all the information available.

The 9/11 Commission acknowledged that while it may be cost prohibitive to replace all IC department and agency networks with a single network, technology could be used to implement a search function that would work across all network domains, allowing an analyst to see that information was available without having to make requests in the blind.

Cybersecurity Organization and Recommendation #3: Assessment

The challenge of information sharing within the IC endures to this day, but they do not diminish the relevance of the 9/11 Commission's recommendation. The recent Wikileaks scandal and alleged involvement of army Private Bradley Manning is an example of the pitfalls in making information widely accessible. Manning is accused of downloading thousands of classified documents unrelated to his work as an intelligence analyst and then providing them to Wikileaks.[114]

While the research did not use classified information, it is reasonable to assume that this problem exists within the cybersecurity community as well. *The Homeland Security Act* and HSPD-7 established a supported/supporting relationship that should encourage information sharing. However, this relationship has been slow to grow. It was not until 2010 that a memorandum of agreement on cybersecurity support was exchanged between DOD and DHS. This memorandum is significant because it more clearly defines the level of support each department will provide the other. Because of the memorandum, DHS located its Director for Cybersecurity Coordination at the National Security Agency

---

[114]Charlie, Savage, "Private Accused of Leaks Offers Partial Guilty Plea," *The New York Times*, http://www.nytimes.com/2012/11/09/us/army-private-in-wikileaks-case-offers-partial-guilty-plea.html (accessed November 14, 2012).

to act as a liaison to NSA and USCYBERCOM. DHS also assigned individuals to work as NSA within a Joint Coordination Element, NSA's Directorate of Acquisition, NSA/CSS' Threat Operations Center (one of six cybersecurity centers). It also assigned representatives from DHS's Office of the General Counsel and Office for Civil Rights and Civil Liberties to support the Directory for Cybersecurity Coordination.[115] In return, NSA (DOD) detailed a senior executive-level person to work at the Joint Coordination Element, identified legal counterparts to work with DHS' representatives, and established a Cryptologic Services Group at DHS's NCCIC to support DHS' cybersecurity efforts and the *National Cyber Incident Response Plan*.[116] The memorandum tasked USCYBERCOM with locating a Cyber Support Element at the NCCIC and required DOD (NSA and USCYBERCOM) and DHS to conduct joint operational planning.[117] This memorandum of agreement was an important step in increasing interdepartmental cooperation. But without a more complete study and access to sensitive cyber security operations, such as the monthly oversight meetings called for in the DOD/DHS memorandum, it is unknown how well information is shared between DHS, DOD and DOJ and other cyber agencies.

---

[115]Department of Defense, *Memorandum of Agreement Between The Department of Homeland Security and the Department of Defense Regarding Cybersecurity* (Washington, DC: Government Printing Office, 2010), 1-3.

[116]Ibid., 3-4.

[117]Ibid., 4.

Recommendation #5: Organizing America's Defenses in the United States

The 9/11 Commission also discussed the FBI's future role and its relevance to national security. As part of this discussion, the Commission cautioned against taking away the FBI's intelligence mission and giving it to a newly created domestic intelligence agency. The Commission argued against this course of action. If implemented, it would incur great costs in terms of time, infrastructure and money. It could also be detrimental to the FBI's capacity and capability. The Commission also noted that the FBI's combination of law enforcement and intelligence missions already gives it the tools and IC connections necessary to prosecute targets in an efficient manner. While the role of law enforcement and intelligence are separate, the FBI uses both in a mutually supportive manner. For example, information gathered under the auspices of law enforcement can be used to inform the intelligence arena as well. This unique combination of capabilities and authorities is an asset and justifies the FBI's continued role in national security.

Cybersecurity Organization and Recommendation #5: Assessment

Establishing a new domestic intelligence agency is a pertinent concern. At what point would a centralized cyber entity be a natural progression of cybersecurity? Has the topic of "cyber" matured enough at the national strategy and policy level? Have offensive and defensive capabilities arrived at a point where they could be considered analogous to kinetic weapons? The latter is an important point of comparison within military circles. If cyber weapons achieved by capability/capacity and reliability comparable to kinetic weapons it would demonstrate maturity of cyber as a warfighting domain, one whose organization might need reevaluating. With the cybersecurity organization currently distributed between three separate departments, does the U.S. need a centralized entity that has a singular focus on U.S. cyber capabilities? Would such an entity be worth the additional resources it would take to create and operate? Could it take advantage of the "joint-mindedness" advocated by the 9/11 Commission? Could the personnel currently assigned to execute the US cyber mission be assigned to such an entity while remaining in the employ of their home service, department or agency in order to reduce costs and duplication of effort?

Third-party Opinion

While independent review and analysis the existing policy documents reveals key insights to the progression (or lack thereof) of cybersecurity efforts, it is important to acknowledge contributions in this area by other entities. Several reputable think tanks have produced important analyses on cybersecurity. The Center for Strategic and International Studies, and the Atlantic Council, two non-partisan groups, are among the organizations that have made noteworthy contributions.

Center for Strategic and International Studies

CSIS is a key contributor in the national discussion on cybersecurity and has set up a special cybersecurity commission that has issued two important documents on the subject. These include *Securing Cyberspace for the 44th Presidency* and *Cybersecurity Two Years Later.* The commission also participated in president Obama's Cyberspace Policy Review.

Securing Cyberspace for the 44th Presidency

CSIS began work on what became *Securing Cyberspace for the 44th Presidency* in 2007. The document takes a comprehensive look at cybersecurity policy and organization. The commission's findings and recommendations can be found below (see table 10).[118] Of these recommendations, several have already been adopted or incorporated by the Obama administration, including the *National Strategy for Trusted Identities in Cyberspace*, *International Strategy for Cyberspace*, and *National Initiative for Cybersecurity Education*.

Table 10.   Findings and Recommendations-Securing Cyberspace for the 44th Presidency

Findings		
1. Cybersecurity is now a major national security problem for the United States	2. Decisions and actions must respect privacy and civil liberties	3. Only a comprehensive national security strategy that embraces both the domestic and international aspects of cybersecurity will make us more secure
Recommendations		
1. Create a comprehensive national security strategy for cyberspace		
2. Lead from the White House		
3. Reinvent the public-private partnership		
4. Regulate cyberspace		
5. Authenticate digital identities		
6. Modernize authorities		
7. Use acquisitions policy to improve security		
8. Build capabilities		
9. Do not start over		

Source: Center for Strategic and International Studies, *Securing Cyberspace for the 44th Presidency* (Washington, DC: Center for Strategic and International Studies, 2008), 1-3.

---

[118]Center for Strategic and International Studies, *Securing Cyberspace for the 44th Presidency* (Washington, DC: Center for Strategic and International Studies, 2008), 1-2.

Of special relevance within this document is the recommendations and focus on the nation's cyber organization. Specifically, the commission recommended the president establish an assistant for cyberspace. Obama created the position of Cybersecurity Coordinator. Counter to the commission's recommendation, however, this coordinator position falls in line with the "czar" model used in modern presidencies. The commission did not approve of a czar position, citing its lack of powers to exercise programmatic oversight. These two recommendations mirror this study's conclusions. Additionally, the commission concluded that because cybersecurity has expanded beyond homeland security and protecting critical infrastructure, it required a new organizational structure. The commission understood that effective cybersecurity strategy also required including international efforts, military capabilities, and intelligence.[119] This influenced further recommendations by CSIS for cybersecurity coordination to move from DHS to the White House. Specifically, the commission recommended the White House establish a cybersecurity directorate within the National Security Council, as well as a national office for cyberspace with a staff to assist the assistant for cyberspace. These recommendations were wholly declined, which has contributed to a lack of unity of effort within the cybersecurity organization.

Cybersecurity Two Years Later

In 2010, the same CSIS commission followed up its *Securing Cyberspace for the 44th Presidency* with *Cybersecurity Two Years Later*. In it, the commission cites the advancements made in cybersecurity, in part because of its contributions via *Securing*

---

[119]Ibid., 35.

Cyberspace for the 44th Presidency and Obama's *Cyberspace Policy Review*, but also criticizes the reduced power of the president's cybersecurity coordinator and missed opportunities to establish a more powerful federal cybersecurity entity. Specifically, the commission was surprised when it observed federal agencies seeking to protect their roles in cybersecurity out of selfish need rather for than good of the nation during the Cyberspace Policy Review.[120]

The commission also criticized past strategic documents for being primarily a collection of generalized goals and called for the federal government to avoid rehashing what it perceived as a flawed 2003 *National Strategy to Secure Cyberspace.* The document advocated using the objectives contained within *Securing Cyberspace for the 44th Presidency* and the *Cyberspace Policy* Review, while assigning "timelines and responsibilities for achieving them."[121]

Unlike The Heritage Foundation, and other think tanks who argue against federally mandated cybersecurity, the commission is critical of Clinton and G.W. Bush administration cybersecurity policies that were based on information sharing and partnership between the federal government and the private sector. The document argues that this policy is flawed because of three reasons: (1) private entities will not freely share information because of liability, antitrust and business competition risks; (2) sharing

---

[120]Center for Strategic and International Studies, *Cybersecurity Two Years Later* (Washington, DC: Center for Strategic and International Studies, 2010), 4.

[121]Ibid., 6.

classified data with industry is enormously difficult; and (3) concerned parties will not

always take action.[122]

In this document the commission advocated for a more robust federal

cybersecurity role and suggests ten areas where this should occur (see table 11)

Table 11.   Recommended Focus Areas-Cyberspace Two Years Later
Coherent organization and leadership for federal efforts for cybersecurity and recognition of cybersecurity as a national priority.
Clear authority to mandate better cybersecurity in critical infrastructure and develop new ways to work with the private sector.
A foreign policy that uses all tools of U.S. power to create norms, new approaches to governance, and consequences for malicious actions in cyberspace. The new policy should lay out a vision for the future of the global Internet.
An expanded ability to use intelligence and military capabilities for defense against advanced foreign threats.
Strengthened oversight for privacy and civil liberties, with clear rules and processes adapted to digital technologies.
Improve authentication of identity for critical infrastructure.
Build an expanded workforce with adequate cybersecurity skills.
Change federal acquisition policy to drive the market toward more secure products and services.
A revised policy and legal framework to guide government cybersecurity actions.
Research and development (R&D) focused on the hard problems of cybersecurity and a process to identify these problems and allocate funding in a coordinated manner.

Source: Center for Strategic and International Studies, *Cyberspace Two Years Later* (Washington, DC: Center for Strategic and International Studies, 2010), 5-14.

In conclusion, the commission maintained the relevance of its recommendations

from 2010 while reiterating that centerpieces of previous cyber policies: (1) public-

private partnership; (2) information sharing; and (3) self-regulation had all proven

---

[122]Ibid., 3.

themselves unsuccessful strategies. Despite emphasizing the nation's need to undertake strong cybersecurity reforms now, CSIS acknowledged that in discussions with analysts and senior Washington-based officials there was belief that it would take a cyber-9/11 or catastrophic cyber event to take action.[123]

Atlantic Council

Cyber Security: An Integrated Government Strategy for Progress

Cyber Security: An Integrated Government Strategy for Progress is different than other documents written by cybersecurity advocates. Rather than assuming that cybersecurity can be "achieved," this document begins with the premise that the cybersecurity challenge is actually "reducing cyber insecurity."[124] It also categorizes the cyber threat differently than any other organization, choosing to use only two categories: (1) those with potential national security consequences and (2) those with criminal objectives.[125]

The document argues that the government must play a strong role in three areas:

1. Ensuring that the Department of Defense (DOD) and the Intelligence Community (IC) can operate effectively while under cyber attack, including in wartime.

2. Ensuring through effective public-private partnerships that key critical infrastructures-electrical grid, financial, telecommunications and

---

[123]Ibid., 15.

[124]Franklin D. Kramer, *Cyber Security: An Integrated Governmental Strategy for Progress* (Washington, DC: Atlantic Council, 2010), 2.

[125]Ibid.

governmental-do not suffer catastrophic failure if attacked, and can maintain/return to adequate service while under attack.

3. Limiting espionage and exfiltration of national security information.[126]

The document's discussion on DOD is particularly interesting because of its recommendations for how DOD should be pursuing cyber related activities, its criticism for how DOD is currently treats cyber issues, particularly CNA, and for addressing potential U.S. responses to cyber attacks.

The first two items are both areas where DOD strategies (NDS, NMS, NMS-CO), are lacking. First, the document stated that the main challenges are: (1) designing, deploying and operating effective capabilities; (2) training against cyber attacks; and (3) developing (and then deploying) better future capabilities.[127] While non-specific as to "capabilities," the repetition of these capabilities in items 1 and 3 recognize that cyber capabilities have limited "shelf-life" and that the design and implementation of cyber capabilities is a continual process. This is an important concept that other strategies and documents either do not consider, or assume is going to happen automatically.

Second, this document was also critical of DOD's integration of CNA capabilities into normal operational capabilities, stating that it suffered from incorrectly limiting CNA to strictly wartime use and over-classifying CNA capabilities.[128] While this research largely avoided discussion of CNA due to classification constraints, the application of CNA is another concept that is lacking from DOD or national-level strategies. Strategic

---

[126]Ibid., 1.

[127]Ibid., 3.

[128]Ibid., 4.

documents not only inform its intended audience, they also serve as strategic communications devices for one's adversaries. By limiting discussion on intended uses of cyber capabilities, this document highlights a shortcoming within current cyber strategy and policy. If the U.S. would more clearly articulate and expanded upon its intended use of CNA, it could serve to have a deterrent effect, thereby enhancing overall U.S. cybersecurity.

Lastly, four escalating responses levels were offered in the event of a cyber attacks:

1. First level: Bilateral diplomatic

2. Second level: International diplomacy (e.g. United Nations)

3. Third level: Economic sanctions (e.g. follow non-proliferation examples)

4. Fourth level: Cyber or Kinetic weapon response[129]

These recommendations are conceptually unique among cybersecurity discussion reviewed during the course of this research. The concept of retaliation is only addressed tangentially in DOD strategic documents and did not specifically address either cyber attacks against the U.S. or specific responses that would be employed. The responses advocated by this document advance the discussion on cybersecurity because they seek to bring CNA into the realm of "regular" weapons. While CNA capabilities remain unknown, there is potential that their use will be considered more "acceptable" than current kinetic weapons, thereby increasing the likelihood of their use. Cyber weapons have already allegedly been used by nation-states in war; the Israelis' use against the

---

[129]Ibid., 5.

Syrian during the bombing of their nuclear facility is one example.[130] By placing cyber weapons on par with kinetic weapons, the document seeks to enhance the dialogue and discussion on the nationwide impacts CNA can have.

---

[130]Richard A. Clarke and Robert K. Knake, *Cyber War: The Next Threat to National Security* (New York: Harper Collins Publishers, 2010), 5-6.

CHAPTER 5

CONCLUSIONS AND RECOMMENDATIONS

Conclusions

Despite the USG's efforts to address cyber security over the last 17 years, an effective cybersecurity strategy, policy and organization continues to elude the nation. Because of rapidly evolving technology, and the cost of implementing changes across expansive government architecture, cybersecurity is a complex and difficult problem. Coupled with evolving government foci, and a complex bureaucratic environment (legislative and organizational), the USG has not developed its cybersecurity strategy or policy, or postured its cyber organization for a post-9/11 environment. As a result, the United States remains vulnerable to a devastating cyber attack.

Technology

Rapidly evolving technology has inhibited strategy, policy and organizational development. The USG has two different problem sets that make achieving a sustainable cybersecurity difficult, but achievable. First, the price of technology continues to fall. This allows individuals, groups, or states to engage in cyberspace operations more easily than the past.[131] As a result, the number of potential threats to U.S. cybersecurity continues to expand. A subset of this technological problem is that software sophistication mirrors the computing power of hardware. The marriage of powerful

---

[131]Chairman, Joint Chiefs of Staff, JP 1-02, *Department of Defense Dictionary of Military and Associated Terms*, 83.

computers with sophisticated software increases the ability of hostile groups to target US critical infrastructure.

The second problem with technology is the vast nature of the US cyber architecture and the cost incurred through daily operation and maintenance. While the price of technology continues to decrease, it is not feasible for the US to upgrade all hardware simultaneously. DOD alone maintains approximately "7 million machines and 15,000 networks."[132] Because of this gap, vulnerabilities due to antiquated hardware are perpetuated. Additionally, cybersecurity organization components might lack access to technology that would allow them to fulfill their mission more efficiently and effectively. Linked with the rapidly evolving technology and software problem is the need for a skilled workforce. The entire USG workforce needs cybersecurity training. This could be as simple as the yearly computer-based instruction mandated of military members using DOD computer networks. For cybersecurity professionals, the highly technical nature of their field makes them very expensive to train. Network administrators, for example, may require up to five or more years experience prior to acceptance into the Microsoft Certified Master Program, the highest certification tier (of 3) that Microsoft offers.[133] CISCO has a three-tier program for their network security certifications. The lower two tiers require recertification every three years. The top tier recommends 3-5 years of experience prior to seeking "expert certification," which costs $1,500 for a two-part exam

---

[132]Franklin D. Kramer, *Cyber Security: An Integrated Governmental Strategy for Progress*, 3.

[133]Microsoft, "Microsoft Certified Master Program," Microsoft Learning, http://www.microsoft.com/learning/en/us/certification/master.aspx (accessed November 14, 2012).

(2-hour written exam and 8-hour practical lab exam). The lab portion requires travel to a CICSO lab, incurring additional costs to the individual or employer seeking this qualification.[134] Assuming a 20-year career, a network security professional could spend more than 25 percent of their career just attaining expert certification. This also assumes no major hardware or software changes that would necessitate new training or certifications. To put this into military terms, a naval aviator or SEAL can be fully trained and qualified in less than half the time.

Changing Government Focus

The Clinton administration demonstrated a remarkable awareness of cyber-related threats to critical infrastructure. Through PDDs 39, 63 and the PCCIP, Clinton established ambitious cybersecurity goals. Cyber issues featured prominently within subsequent national security documents and despite the relative infancy of the cyberspace domain, the administration was keen to establish the infrastructure, workforce, and collaborative relationship with the private sector necessary to achieve credible cybersecurity.

Despite the positive start and ambitious goals of the Clinton administration, the 9/11 terrorist attacks stalled cyber initiatives. The Bush administration was squarely focused on countering domestic and international terrorism. It viewed critical infrastructure protection through a counterterrorism lens. Despite the heavy focus on

---

[134]CISCO, "CISCO CCIE Security," CCIE Security Track, http://www.cisco.com/web/learning/le3/ccie/security/index.html (accessed November 14, 2012); CISCO, "Lab Exam," The CISCO Learning Network, https://learningnetwork.cisco.com/community/certifications/ccie_security/lab_exam?tab=take-your-lab-exam (accessed November 14, 2012).

counterterrorism, the Bush administration made positive progress in the cybersecurity realm. The Comprehensive National Cybersecurity Initiative contained within National Security Presidential Directive (NSPD)-54/Homeland Security Presidential Directive (HSPD-23: *Cyber Security and Monitoring* was one example., Strategies such as *The National Strategy for the Physical Protection of Critical Infrastructures and Key Assets*, and *The National Strategy to Secure Cyberspace* all advanced USG cybersecurity efforts. Overall, progress during the Bush administration was uneven. Other nation-level strategic documents were inconsistent in advancing cybersecurity awareness, strategy and policy.

Bureaucratic Inertia

Since the 1990s, the USG has published numerous strategic documents. Some have focused entirely on critical infrastructure protection or cybersecurity. While this demonstrates an awareness of the continued importance of cybersecurity, progress in achieving the goals within the documents has been slow. For instance, in 2000, the NPISP called upon the USG to build strong cybersecurity foundations through trained professionals. This need was echoed three years later in the NSSC. Manning and training shortfalls were cited again seven years later in Obama's CNCI and again in CSIS' *A Human Capital Strategy in Cybersecurity*. In advocating for rigorous certification process for cybersecurity professionals, CSIS stated, "In many ways, cybersecurity is similar to like 19th medicine-a growing field dealing with real threats with lots of self-taught practitioners only some of whom know what they are doing."[135] Despite being termed as

---

[135]Center for Strategic and International Studies, *A Human Capital Strategy for Cybersecurity: Technical Proficiency Matters* (Washington, DC: Center for Strategic and International Studies, 2010), 3.

the essential ingredient for cybersecurity within these documents, there has been no rapid implementation of a coherent workforce strategy.[136] One might expect DOD to be the most responsive federal department; however, the first services to create cyber-specific specialties (navy and air force) did not do so until a decade later after the NPISP.

Shifting cybersecurity visions have also slowed progress. Both the Clinton and Bush administrations stated that government could not be a single-source solution for national cybersecurity. Both held that the government not effectively legislate cybersecurity. They also stressed the need for public and private sectors to collaborate to achieve this goal. This attitude shifted within both Congress and the Obama administration in 2012. Congress failed to pass comprehensive cybersecurity legislation that would have mandated the private sector meet minimum federal cybersecurity standards. In lieu of legislation, the Obama administration is drafting an executive order to mandate national cybersecurity standards.

While an executive order may achieve relatively quick results, they can be transitory and exacerbate political disagreements on courses of action. Even if President Obama enacts an executive order, it is only certain to be in effect for as long as he is in office. The next president could overturn or amend the executive order upon assuming office. Additionally, by pursuing an executive order, Obama risks conflict with Congress. The body has a tendency to view executive orders as an "end-run" around its legislative authorities and it could pass legislation that contradicts the executive order later.

Outside analysis has postulated that government regulation of cybersecurity could be harmful. Three main reasons are offered in this analysis:

---

[136]White House, *National Plan for Information Systems Protection*, v.

1. Slow innovation

2. Regulations cannot keep pace with cyberspace

3. Compliance over collaboration[137]

Cybersecurity regulations, whether enacted through legislation or executive order could have the above effects. First, rather than develop new ways to bolster cybersecurity, companies will work toward government-approved measures that may be inadequate or less efficient. Second, the rapid development of and dynamic nature of cyberspace will make it difficult for legislation to keep pace. If the nearly decade-old *The National Strategy to Secure Cyberspace* is any indication, this objection to regulation has merit. Third, regulation will only induce minimum-level compliance. This could have the unintended consequence of making companies less safe as they spend precious resources attaining government compliance that cannot "guarantee" cybersecurity.[138]

Suboptimal Organization

The USG organization hampers cybersecurity. Similar to the IC, the U.S. cybersecurity organization spans multiple departments and agencies. This has resulted in an unwieldy division of labor between DHS, DOD, and DOJ (FBI). While the respective focus of each department makes sense, no single entity can claim to have a holistic view of the cybersecurity organization. Each department has control over one or more Cybersecurity Centers, some acting as 24/7 watch centers. The NCCIC is responsible for

---

[137]Paul Rosenzweig, "Congress Should Not Enable Executive Orders on Cybersecurity," The Heritage Foundation, http://www.heritage.org/research/reports/2012/09/cybersecurity-regulation-regulatory-approach-is-wrong (accessed November 14, 2012).

[138]Ibid.

maintaining the national cyber common operational picture; however, it does not generate information on its own and is reliant upon the six cybersecurity centers to supply it with data. This clearinghouse approach is not without merit, but without control over the people and resources capable of generating cyber information and intelligence, the NCCIC will continue to operate below its potential.

The cybersecurity organization is unbalanced. The lion's share of expertise and resources lay within DOD. The service cyber organizations are comprised of approximately 43,000. This is equivalent in size to nearly 23 percent of the total DHS workforce.[139] The department also appears to have the most integrated internal cyber organization. DHS and FBI also have mature cyber organizations; however, DOD's cyber architecture includes individual services and joint combatant commanders on multiple levels. With the exception of the Coast Guard (DHS), each service has a command designated as a service component to USCYBERCOM. Each of these commands includes numerous subcomponents. DOD and the FBI also integrate their intelligence and cyber functions. For example, the Director of NSA is dual-hatted as Commander, USCYBERCOM. This integration yields efficiencies in both personnel and responsiveness. The FBI cyber organization contains cyber intelligence units aligned by regional focus and expertise. While the FBI is primarily focused on law enforcement, they are a member of the IC and have a counterintelligence role in cybersecurity.

---

[139]Sydney J. Freedberg Jr., "Cyber Commands Pushing Shift from IT Workers to 'Warriors'," Aol Defense, http://www.defense.aol.com/2012/07/26/service-cyber-commands-shift-from-web-geeks-to-warriors (accessed November 19, 2012); Alice Lipowicz, "Huge size of DHS contractor workforce leaves senators 'astonished'," FCW: The Business of Federal Technology, http://www.fcw.com/articles/2010/03/01/dhs-has-too-many-contract-employees-senators-charge.aspx (accessed November 19, 2012).

The cybersecurity organization suffers from lack of unified leadership. Despite the HSA's best efforts to establish a supported/supporting relationship between DHS as cybersecurity lead and the rest of the federal government, the construct is not as successful as DOD's joint arena. The cybersecurity organization has yet to follow the IC example. The DNI position allowed the IC to control budgets, priorities, and lines of effort. Without this unity of command, the cybersecurity organization will continue to resemble the mythical hydra–multiple heads with no one in charge.

Recommendations

Primary Recommendations

More research on this subject is needed. There are so many facets to the topic of U.S. cybersecurity; a single research thesis cannot adequately cover all subtopics. Further research into the U.S. cybersecurity strategy, policy and organization should be focused along the following lines:

1. Classified research into this subject should seek to validate or refute the study's findings. Because this research is focused on strategy, policy, and organization and not on actual cyber capacity or capabilities, expanding the research to include documents classified up to the Secret level should prove adequate and enlightening. The National Military Strategy for Cyberspace Operations was classified Secret, while a pre-decisional draft of an Obama administration Cybersecurity Executive Order was Unclassified/For Official Use Only.

2. Critical Infrastructure and potential cyber impacts

3. Assess legislative or Executive Order impacts

4. Incorporate international components

5. Assess the responsibilities, and contributions of state and local government, academia and private industry to U.S. cybersecurity.

Recommendation #1

While conducting classified research restricts the audience, this additional information provides a more accurate assessment of the cybersecurity community. During the course of this research, several key policy documents were unavailable or had significant portions redacted. Those documents might contain information that could have altered this research's conclusions or validated its findings. The aforementioned draft Obama administration Cybersecurity Executive Order was reported to be at the Unclassified/For Official Use Only level, while *The National Military Strategy for Cyberspace Operations* was classified Secret. Specifically, the NMS-CO contained redacted information about how DOD classified the cybersecurity threat. This information might be valuable in assessing if strategy, policy, and organization were postured to meet those threats. Classified documentation might provide additional insight into how the cybersecurity organization was actually functioning. That aspect of organization evaluation was not undertaken in this study.

Recommendation #2

While this research identified critical infrastructure and its relationship to cybersecurity, further research needs to assess the impact of cybersecurity, or the lack thereof, on critical infrastructure. Because of the increasing links critical infrastructure has with cyberspace, it is difficult to discuss critical infrastructure without discussing cybersecurity. Likewise, discussing cybersecurity requires discussing its impact on society, to include critical infrastructure. This study did not incorporate extensive research into the documented costs cyber attacks have had on society, though many references to monetary costs existed. Future studies should collate evidence of documented attacks and incorporate cost data when available to show the repercussions of poor cybersecurity. Specifically, CSIS publishes a running list entitled *Significant Cyber Incidents Since 2006*, which includes incidents such as the hacking of DOS networks, (2006), Israeli disruption of Syrian air defense networks (2007), and several oil companies reporting loss of corporate intelligence data (2008).[140]

Recommendation #3

The legislative process needs more attention. What is or should be Congress's role in cyber security? If the Obama administration opts to do a congressional work around by issuing an executive order, what are the effects on future cyber security? What are the implications for the private sector (to include secondary and tertiary effects)? The Bush and Clinton administrations were adamantly opposed to federal management of national cybersecurity and put in place several initiatives to foster cybersecurity collaboration between the public and private sectors. If either Congress of the President enacts federal regulations, future studies can compare and contrast the effectiveness of pre-Obama cybersecurity efforts to determine which system performed better.

---

[140] Andrew Lewis, "*Significant Cyber Incidents Since 2006*," Center for Strategic and International Studies, http://www.csis.org/publication/cyber-events-2006 (accessed November 19, 2012).

Recommendation #4

International strategies, partnerships, and agreements were deliberately excluded. *The International Strategy for Cyberspace* is one strategy, though this research came upon several references to cybersecurity as a concern of the North Atlantic Treaty Organization and the international community. The research also came upon the alleged use of cyber weapons by the United States and other countries. Further study on this topic should incorporate these items in order to expand the understanding of the U.S. cyber organization, strategy, and policy.

Recommendation #5

State and local governments, academia, and private industry were excluded from this research. The Clinton, Bush, and Obama administrations stated that government echelons below the federal level all have an important role to play in national cybersecurity. Private industry and academia were also acknowledged as having a role in developing tools and knowledge of the cybersecurity arena. Future research should focus on these components of the cyber security world to complement this analysis of the federal echelon.

Secondary Recommendations

Secondary recommendations focus on U.S. cybersecurity strategy, policy, and organization are aligned with a unified cybersecurity strategy, policy, and organization

Recommendation #6-Unified Strategy

The Bush administration's NSSC was a valiant attempt at comprehensive national cybersecurity strategy, however it is almost a decade old and it has not been revised. The document should be revised to include the current U.S. cybersecurity organization and policies and it should evaluate the USG's ability to implement past policies and goals. An updated NSSC should take a holistic view of past strategies and policies and offer an assessment on how those goals have been met.

An updated NSSC should be added to the list of congressionally mandated strategies to ensure currency. In this way, the executive branch will be responsible for updating cybersecurity security in addition to other priorities (i.e. counterterrorism).

Recommendation #7-Unified Policy

An updated NSSC should also unify the federal cyber architecture. Today, each federal department or agency maintains its own cybersecurity standards. For example, DOD is responsible for its own classified and unclassified networks. A single entity should be empowered to ensure compliance with cybersecurity policy across the federal government. If the federal government cannot maintain a single standard, how can it expect private industry to do so?

Recommendation #8-Unified Organization

Just as the IC now has a single executive to manage the IC budget and priorities, so too must the cyber organization. The cyber threat can cause significant damage to the nation's critical infrastructure. The US cyber organization must keep pace with that rapidly evolving threat. A cabinet-level cybersecurity executive would be more effective than the current cyber-czar would if the position possesses the necessary authority to make the organization more efficient and effective.

As cyber issues continue to mature, such a position might be on par with DNI in status, a Director of National Cybersecurity (DNCS). In the interim, many of the roles, responsibilities and authorities of a DNCS could be handled under the auspices of the DNI's office as a Deputy Director position. This deputy director position could rotate among top DHS, DOD, and DOJ cyber professionals.

The cyber organization would also need to change as cyber issues mature. Like the IC, the cybersecurity organization is an interagency organism. In line with instituting a DNCS position, a joint, COCOM-like entity should be created as the DNCS staff. Led by the DNCS, it would be manned by cyber professionals trained by the constituent organizations with cybersecurity roles: DHS, DOD, DOJ, and other federal departments and agencies. While assigned to the DNCS staff, they would be managed and evaluated by DNCS leadership. In this way, the DNCS could have a robust headquarters staff to include the NCCIC (or successor watch center; a National Cybersecurity Operations Center). This operations center would be responsible for both civil and defense related cyber situational awareness.

Creating and managing a national cybersecurity staff in this way would free the DNCS from the burden of owning, managing and paying for all cyber professionals in the government. It would also allow DHS, DOD, and DOJ to continue focusing on areas specific to their US Code Title authorities. The DOD executing a cyber operation overseas is one example (see figure 4).

Summary

A few recommendations could assist in transforming the cybersecurity organization into an agile, responsive, and efficient enterprise. The organization is fashioned on a pre-9/11IC model. The DHS Secretary is akin to the pre-9/11 role of the DCI. She is a department head, the leader of the cyber enterprise and advisor to the president. Unlike the DCI, however, she has a multi-faceted mission. Additionally, while she has many powers invested in her, Secretary Napolitano lacks control over the resources and budgets that define the capacity and capability of the cyber enterprise. This lack of control goes beyond just money, but includes personnel standards (training, assignments, etc.). Finally, the cyber organization spans multiple departments and agencies as the IC does. The IC is still made of multiple intelligence agencies; however, the cyber enterprise is concentrated in three departments. This should make the organization more agile, responsive, and efficient, but the decade old HSA and HSPD-7 need continual updates to modernize the supported/supporting relationship between departments.

National cybersecurity awareness began over 17 years ago in the Clinton administration. Several cyber security centric strategies have been developed and cyber concerns are found throughout the NSS, NDS, and NMS. Despite these strategies, progress is uneven. Many documents repeat the statements of their predecessors. Those documents that have stated goals or timelines, such as PDD-63, do not receive follow-through in achieving those aims. In sum, the necessary steps to ensure cybersecurity either remain the same, or are exacerbated as the country falls behind the advance of its adversaries' capabilities.

Similar to strategy and policy, the cybersecurity organization has failed to advance with changing times. Individual components, whether uniformed service or department-level, may operate well. Unfortunately, cyber security policy has created a system where component organizations may experience success, but interagency collaboration is not effectively defined. Interagency cooperation is a prerequisite for nationwide success, but this aspect of the cybersecurity organization will continue to suffer because support to a separate department will remain a secondary priority in a non-crisis situation. Until changes similar to those recommended here are implemented, the cyber organization will continue to operate in a sub-optimized fashion

Several factors explain the delays in advancing a robust national cybersecurity effort, one such factor was the post-9/11 counterterrorism focus. Differing visions and opinions of several presidential administrations also delayed or altered ongoing efforts. Unfortunately, a slowly maturing strategy, policy, and organization will do nothing to slow the growing number of adversaries with cyber capabilities, nor will it deter them from seeking to use cyberspace as a medium to threaten the country. Without dramatic and measurable change along the lines proposed here, the USG cybersecurity strategy, policy, and organization will continue to leave the nation vulnerable to a devastating cyber attack.

ILLUSTRATIONS

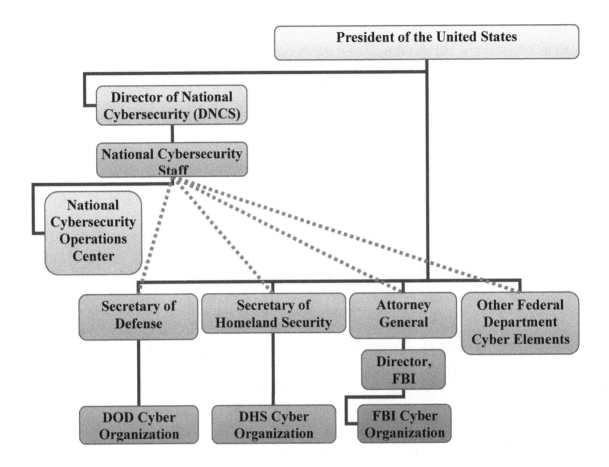

Figure 4.   Recommended Cyber Security Organization

Source: Compiled by author.

114

GLOSSARY

24th Air Force. The operational warfighting organization that establishes, operates, maintains and defends Air Force networks to ensure warfighters can maintain the information advantage as US forces prosecute military operations around the world. Air Force service component of USCYBERCOM.[141]

Computer Network Attack. Action taken through the use of computer networks to disrupt, deny, degrade, or destroy information resident in computers and computer networks, or the computers and networks themselves. Also called CNA.[142]

Computer Network Defense. Actions taken to protect, monitor, analyze, detect, and respond to unauthorized activity within the Department of Defense information systems and computer networks. Also called CND.[143]

Computer Network Exploitation. Enabling operations and intelligence collection capabilities conducted through the use of computer networks to gather data from target or adversary automated information systems or networks. Also called CNE.[144]

Computer Network Operations. Comprised of computer network attack, computer network defense, and related computer network exploitation enabling operations. Also called CNO.[145]

Critical Infrastructure. Those systems and assets, both physical and cyber, so vital to the Nation [United States] that their incapacity or destruction would have a debilitating impact on national security, national economic security, and/or national public health and safety.[146]

Cyber Counterintelligence. Measures to identify, penetrate, or neutralize foreign operations that use cyber means as the primary tradecraft methodology, as well as

---

[141]24th Air Force, "24th Air Force Fact Sheet," http://www.24af.af.mil/library/factsheets/factsheet.asp?id=15663 (accessed November 19, 2012).

[142]Chairman, Joint Chiefs of Staff, JP 1-02, *Department of Defense Dictionary of Military and Associated Terms*, 65.

[143]Ibid.

[144]Ibid.

[145]Ibid., 66.

[146]White House, *National Plan for Information Systems Protection*, vi.

foreign intelligence service collection efforts that use traditional methods to gauge cyber capabilities and intentions.[147]

Cybersecurity. Measures taken to protect a computer or computer system (as on the Internet) against unauthorized access or attack.[148]

Cyberspace. A global domain within the information environment consisting of the interdependent network of information technology infrastructures, including the Internet, telecommunications networks, computer systems, and embedded processors and controllers.[149]

Electromagnetic Spectrum. The range of frequencies of electromagnetic radiation from zero to infinity. It is divided into 26 alphabetically designated bands.[150]

Electronic Attack. Division of electronic warfare involving the use of electromagnetic energy, directed energy, or antiradiation weapons to attack personnel, facilities, or equipment with the intent of degrading, neutralizing, or destroying enemy combat capability and is considered a form of fires. Also called EA.[151]

Electronic Protection. Division of electronic warfare involving actions taken to protect personnel, facilities, and equipment from any effects of friendly or enemy use of the electromagnetic spectrum that degrade, neutralize, or destroy friendly combat capability. Also called EP.[152]

Electronic Warfare. Military action involving the use of electromagnetic and directed energy to control the electromagnetic spectrum or to attack the enemy. Also called EW.[153]

---

[147]Chairman, Joint Chiefs of Staff, JP 1-02, *Department of Defense Dictionary of Military and Associated Terms*, 83.

[148]Merriam-Webster.com, "Cybersecurity," http://www.merriam-webster.com/ dictionary/cybersecurity (accessed November 4, 2012).

[149]Chairman, Joint Chiefs of Staff, JP 1-02, *Department of Defense Dictionary of Military and Associated Terms,* 83.

[150]Ibid., 107.

[151]Ibid.

[152]Ibid., 108.

[153]Ibid.

Global Information Grid. The globally interconnected, end-to-end set of information capabilities, and associated processes for collecting, processing, storing, disseminating, and managing information on demand to warfighters, policy makers, and support personnel. The Global Information Grid includes owned and leased communications and computing systems and services, software (including applications), data, security services, other associated services and National Security Systems. Also called GIG.[154]

Global Information Infrastructure. The worldwide interconnection of communications networks, computers, databases, and consumer electronics that make vast amounts of information available to users. The global information infrastructure encompasses a wide range of equipment, including cameras, scanners, keyboards, facsimile machines, computers, switches, compact disks, video and audio tape, cable, wire, satellites, fiber-optic transmission lines, networks of all types, televisions, monitors, printers, and much more. The friendly and adversary personnel who make decisions and handle the transmitted information constitute a critical component of the global information infrastructure. Also called GII.[155]

Hacker. A person who illegally gains access to and sometimes tampers with information in a computer system.[156]

Information Operations. 1) The integrated employment, during military operations, of information-related capabilities in concert with other lines of operation to influence, disrupt, corrupt, or usurp the decision-making of adversaries and potential adversaries while protecting our own. Consisting of 5 distinct subcomponents: Computer Network Operations (CNO), Electronic Warfare (EW), Military Deception (MILDEC), Operations Security (OPSEC), Military Information Support Operations (MISO). Also called IO.[157]

Military Deception. Actions executed to deliberately mislead adversary military, paramilitary, or violent extremist organization decision makers, thereby causing the adversary to take specific actions (or inactions) that will contribute to the accomplishment of the friendly mission. Also called MILDEC.[158]

---

[154]Ibid., 138.

[155]Ibid.

[156]Merriam-Webster.com, "Hacker," http://www.merriam-webster.com/dictionary/hacker (accessed November 4, 2012).

[157]Chairman, Joint Chiefs of Staff, JP 1-02, *Department of Defense Dictionary of Military and Associated Terms*, 158.

[158]Ibid., 209.

Military Information Support Operations. Planned operations to convey selected
information and indicators to foreign audiences to influence their emotions,
motives, objective reasoning, and ultimately the behavior of foreign governments,
organizations, groups, and individuals in a manner favorable to the originator's
objectives. Also called MISO.[159]

Network Operations. Activities conducted to operate and defend the Global Information
Grid. Also called NETOPS[160]

Nonlethal Weapons. A weapon that is explicitly designed and primarily employed so as
to incapacitate personnel or materiel, while minimizing fatalities, permanent
injury to personnel, and undesired damage to property and the environment. Also
called NLW.[161]

Operations Security. A process of identifying critical information and subsequently
analyzing friendly actions attendant to military operations and other activities.
Also called OPSEC.[162]

Signals Intelligence. 1) A category of intelligence comprising either individually or in
combination all communications intelligence, electronic intelligence, and foreign
instrumentation signals intelligence, however transmitted. 2) Intelligence derived
from communications, electronic, and foreign instrumentation signals. Also called
SIGINT.[163]

U.S. Army Cyber Command. Army Cyber Command/2nd Army plans, coordinates,
integrates, synchronizes, directs, and conducts network operations and defense of
all Army networks; when directed, conducts cyberspace operations in support of
full spectrum operations to ensure U.S./Allied freedom of action in cyberspace,
and to deny the same to our adversaries. Army service component of
USCYBERCOM. Also called ARCYBER.[164]

U.S. Cyber Command. Is responsible for planning, coordinating, integrating,
synchronizing, and directing activities to operate and defend the Department of

---

[159]Ibid.

[160]Ibid., 230.

[161]Ibid., 232.

[162]Ibid., 244.

[163]Ibid., 299.

[164]United States Army Cyber Command, "U.S. Army Cyber Command/U.S. 2nd
Army," http://www.arcyber.army.mil/org-arcyber.html (accessed November 19, 2012).

Defense information networks and when directed, conduct full-spectrum military cyberspace operations (in accordance with all applicable laws and regulations) in order to ensure U.S. and allied freedom of action in cyberspace, while denying the same to our adversaries. Also called USCYBERCOM.[165]

U.S. Fleet Cyber Command. The mission of Fleet Cyber Command is to serve as central operational authority for networks, cryptologist/signals intelligence, information operations, cyber, electronic warfare, and space capabilities in support of forces afloat and ashore; to direct Navy cyberspace operations globally to deter and defeat aggression and to ensure freedom of action to achieve military objectives in and through cyberspace; to organize and direct Navy cryptologic operations worldwide and support information operations and space planning and operations, as directed; to execute cyber missions as directed; to direct, operate, maintain, secure, and defend the Navy's portion of the Global Information Grid; to deliver integrated cyber, information operations, cryptologic, and space capabilities; to deliver a global Navy cyber common operational picture; to develop, coordinate, assess, and prioritize Navy cyber, cryptologic/signals intelligence, space, information operations, and electronic warfare requirements; to assess Navy cyber readiness; to manage man, train and equip functions associated with Navy Component Commander and Service Cryptologic Commander responsibilities; and to exercise administrative and operational control of assigned forces. Navy service component of USCYBERCOM. Also called FCC.[166]

U.S. Marine Corps Forces Cyber Command. COMMARFORCYBER plans, coordinates, integrates, synchronizes, and directs full spectrum Marine Corps cyberspace operations, to include DoD Global Information Grid Operations, Defensive Cyber Operations, and when directed, plans and executes Offensive Cyberspace Operations, in support of Marine Air Ground Task Force (MAGTF), joint, and combined cyberspace requirements in order to enable freedom of action across all warfighting domains, and deny the same to adversarial forces. Marine Corps service component of USCYBERCOM.[167]

---

[165]United States Strategic Command, "U.S. Cyber Command," http://www.stratcom.mil/factsheets/cyber_command (accessed November 10, 2012).

[166]United States Fleet Cyber Command, "U.S. Fleet Cyber Command/U.S. TENTH Fleet," http://www.fcc.navy.mil (accessed November 19, 2012).

[167]United States Marine Corps Forces Cyber Command, "USMC Cyberspace Update," http://www.afcea-qp.org/luncheons/31Mar11-Bullard-Cyber-Brief.pdf (accessed November 19, 2012).

APPENDIX A

ASSORTED TABLES

The below tables are included here to ease readability in the text and to provide

additional information the reader may find useful.

Table 12. President's Commission on Critical Infrastructure Protection	
Name	Title / Agency
Robert T. Marsh	Chairman
Merritt E. Adams	AT&T
Richard P. Case	IBM
Mary J. Culnan	Georgetown University
Peter H. Daly	Department of the Treasury
John C. Davis	National Security Agency
Thomas J. Falvey	Department of Transportation
Brenton C. Greene	Department of Defense
William J. Harris	Association of American Railroads
David A. Jones	Department of Energy
William B. Joyce	Central Intelligence Agency
David V. Keyes	Federal Bureau of Investigation
Stevan D. Mitchell	Department of Justice
Joseph J. Moorcones	National Security Agency
Irwin M. Pikus	Department of Commerce
William Paul Rodgers, Jr.	National Association of Regulatory Utility Commissioners
Susan V. Simens	Federal Bureau of Investigation
Frederick M. Struble	Federal Reserve Board
Nancy J. Wong	Pacific Gas and Electric Company

Source: Chairman, President's Commission on Critical Infrastructure Protection, *Critical Foundations: Protecting America's Infrastructure-The Report of the President's Commission on Critical Infrastructure Protection* (Washington, DC: Government Printing Office, 1997), iii.

Table 13.	Other Strategic Documents by Presidential Administration	
Clinton	2000	National Plan for Information Systems Protection Version 1.0
Bush	2003	National Strategy to Secure Cyberspace
Bush	2003	The National Strategy for the Physical Protection of Critical Infrastructures and Key Assets
Bush	2006	National Military Strategy for Cyberspace Operations
Bush	2008	NSPD-54/HSPD-23 Comprehensive National Cyberspace Initiative
Obama	2009	Cyberspace Policy Review
Obama	2009	National Infrastructure Protection Plan
Obama	2010	The Comprehensive National Cyberspace Initiative
Obama	2010	National Cyber Incident Response Plan (Interim Version)
Obama	2011	National Strategy for Trusted Identities in Cyberspace
Obama	2011	International Strategy for Cyberspace
Obama	2011	DOD Strategy for Operating in Cyberspace

Source: Compiled by author.

Table 14.	Strategic Guidance for The National Military Strategy for Cyberspace Operations
YEAR	TITLE
2002	*National Strategy for Homeland Security*
2003	HSPD-5, *Management of Domestic Incidents*
2003	HSPD-7, *Critical Infrastructure Identifications*
2003	*National Strategy for the Physical Protection of Critical Infrastructures and Key Assets*
2003	*National Strategy to Secure Cyberspace*
2004	*National Response Plan*
2004	*National Military Strategy*
2004	*DOD Information Assurance Strategic Plan*
2005	Executive Order 13388, *Further Strengthening the Sharing of Terrorism Information to Protect Americans*
2005	*National Defense Strategy*
2005	*Security Cooperation Guidance*
2005	*Strategy for Homeland Defense and Civil Support*
2006	*Unified Command Plan*
2006	*National Security Strategy*
2006	*Quadrennial Defense Review*
Unknown	Unknown (Redacted in partially declassified release)
Unknown	Unknown (Redacted in partially declassified release)

Source: Chairman, Joint Chiefs of Staff, *The National Military Strategy for Cyberspace Operations* (Washington, DC: Government Printing Office, 2006), B-1.

Table 15. Categorizing the Cyber Threat (DHS, DOD, FBI)				
DHS	**DOD**			**FBI**
4 Threat Categories	**6 Threat Categories**	**6 Threat Actors**	**7 Vulnerabilities**	**3 Threat Categories**
Individual	**Traditional**-Threats arise from states employing recognized military capabilities and forces in well-understood forms of military conflict.		**Architecture**-The current cyberspace architecture is permissive to the conduct of malicious activity.	Organized Crime
Criminal	**Irregular**-Threats can use cyberspace as an unconventional asymmetric means to counter traditional advantages.		**Operating with Partners**-Connecting to partner components of cyberspace, introduces additional vulnerabilities.	
Terrorist	**Catastrophic**-Threats involve the acquisition, possession, and use of weapons of mass destruction (WMD) or methods producing WMD-like effects.		**Technical Vulnerabilities**-Technical vulnerabilities are an inherent aspect of cyberspace operations.	State-Sponsored
Nation-state	**Disruptive**-Threats are breakthrough technologies that may negate or reduce current US advantages in warfighting domains.	R E D A C T E D	**Commercial Technologies and Outsourcing**- Exploitation could occur anywhere within the technology life-cycle process.	
	Natural-Threats that can damage and disrupt cyberspace include acts of nature such as floods, hurricanes, solar flares, lightning, and tornados.		**Physical Protection**- Insufficient protective measures or poor physical protection procedures.	Terrorist Groups
			Open Source Information- Threat actors may use publicly available information and employ data mining methods to focus intelligence collection efforts and plan attacks against DOD networks.	
	Accidental-Threats are unpredictable and can take many forms.		**Training**-Personnel require thorough training for effective cyberspace operations.	
			Policy Vulnerabilities- Policies are designed to reduce cyberspace vulnerabilities	
			Redacted	
			Redacted	
			Redacted	

Source: Chairman, Joint Chiefs of Staff, *The National Military Strategy for Cyberspace Operations* (Washington, DC: Government Printing Office, 2006), C-1, 2.

Table 16. Cyberspace Policy Review: Near-Term Action Plan
1. Appoint a cybersecurity policy official responsible for coordinating the Nation's cybersecurity policies and activities; establish a strong NSC directorate, under the direction of the cybersecurity policy official dual-hatted to the NSC and the NEC, to coordinate interagency development of cybersecurity-related strategy and policy.
2. Prepare for the President's approval an updated national strategy to secure the information and communications infrastructure. This strategy should include continued evaluation of CNCI activities and, where appropriate, build on its successes.
3. Designate cybersecurity as one of the President's key management priorities and establish performance metrics.
4. Designate a privacy and civil liberties official to the NEC cybersecurity directorate.
5. Convene appropriate interagency mechanisms to conduct interagency-cleared legal analyses of priority cybersecurity-related issues identified during the policy-development process and formulate coherent unified policy guidance that clarifies roles, responsibilities, and the application of agency authorities for cybersecurity-related activities across the federal government.
6. Initiate a national public awareness and education campaign to promote cybersecurity.
7. Develop U.S. Government positions for an international cybersecurity policy framework and strengthen our international partnerships to create initiatives that address the full range of activities, policies, and opportunities associated with cybersecurity.
8. Prepare a cybersecurity incident response plan; initiate a dialog to enhance public-private partnerships with an eye toward streamlining, aligning, and providing resources to optimize their contribution and engagement.
9. In collaboration with other EOP entities, develop a framework for research and development strategies that focus on game-changing technologies that have the potential to enhance the security, reliability, resilience, and trustworthiness of digital infrastructure; provide the research community access to event data to facilitate developing tools, testing theories, and identifying workable solutions.
10. Build a cybersecurity-based identity management vision and strategy that addresses privacy and civil liberties interests, leveraging privacy-enhancing technologies for the Nation.

Source: White House, *Cyberspace Policy Review: Assuring a Trusted and Resilient Information and Communications Infrastructure* (Washington, DC: Government Printing Office, 2009), 37.

Table 17. Cyberspace Policy Review: Mid-Term Action Plan
1. Improve the process for resolution of interagency disagreements regarding interpretations of law and application of policy and authorities for cyber operations.
2. Use the OMB program assessment framework to ensure departments and agencies use performance-based budgeting in pursuing cybersecurity goals.
3. Expand support for key education programs and research and development to ensure the Nation's continued ability to compete in the information age economy.
4. Develop a strategy to expand and train the workforce, including attracting and retaining cybersecurity expertise in the Federal government.
5. Determine the most efficient and effective mechanism to obtain strategic warning, maintain situational awareness, and inform incident response capabilities.
6. Develop a set of threat scenarios and metrics that can be used for risk management decisions, recovery planning, and prioritization of R&D.
7. Develop a process between the government and the private sector to assist in preventing, detecting, and responding to cyber incidents.
8. Develop mechanisms for cybersecurity-related information sharing that address concerns about privacy and proprietary information and make information sharing mutually beneficial.
9. Develop solutions for emergency communications capabilities during a time of natural disaster, crisis, or conflict while ensuring network neutrality.
10. Expand sharing of information about network incidents and vulnerabilities with key allies and seek bilateral and multilateral arrangements that will improve economic and security interests while protecting civil liberties and privacy rights.
11. Encourage collaboration between academic and industrial laboratories to develop migration paths and incentives for the rapid adoption of research and technology development innovations.
12. Use the infrastructure objectives and the research and development framework to define goals for national and international standards bodies.
13. Implement, for high-value activities (e.g., the Smart Grid), an opt-in array of interoperable identity management systems to build trust for online transactions and to enhance privacy.
14. Refine government procurement strategies and improve the market incentives for secure and resilient hardware and software products, new security innovation, and secure managed services.

Source: White House, *Cyberspace Policy Review: Assuring a Trusted and Resilient Information and Communications Infrastructure* (Washington, DC: Government Printing Office, 2009), 38.

BIBLIOGRAPHY

Books

Clarke, Richard A., and Robert K. Knake. *Cyber War: The Next Threat to National Security*. New York: Harper Collins Publishers, 2010.

Government Documents

Chairman, Joint Chiefs of Staff. Joint Publication (JP) 1-02, *Department of Defense Dictionary of Military and Associated Terms*. Washington, DC: Government Printing Office, 2012.

————. *The National Military Strategy for Cyberspace Operations*. Washington, DC: Government Printing Office, 2006.

————. *The National Military Strategy of the United States of America*. Washington, DC: Government Printing Office, 1997.

————. *The National Military Strategy of the United States of America*. Washington, DC: Government Printing Office, 2004.

————. *The National Military Strategy of the United States of America*. Washington, DC: Government Printing Office, 2011.

Chairman, President's Commission on Critical Infrastructure Protection. *Critical Foundations: Protecting America's Infrastructure-The Report of the President's Commission on Critical Infrastructure Protection*. Washington, DC: Government Printing Office, 1997.

Department of Defense. *Memorandum of Agreement Between The Department of Homeland Security and the Department of Defense Regarding Cybersecurity*. Washington, DC: Government Printing Office, 2010.

————. *The National Defense Strategy of the United States of America*. Washington, DC: Government Printing Office, 2005.

————. *National Defense Strategy*. Washington, DC: Government Printing Office, 2008.

————. *Quadrennial Defense Review Report*. Washington, DC: Government Printing Office, 2001.

————. *Quadrennial Defense Review Report*. Washington, DC: Government Printing Office, 2006.

———. *Quadrennial Defense Review Report*. Washington, DC: Government Printing Office, 2010.

———. *Report of the Quadrennial Defense Review*. Washington, DC: Government Printing Office, 1997.

———. *Sustaining U.S. Global Leadership: Priorities for 21st Century Defense*. Washington, DC: Government Printing Office, 2012.

Department of Justice. Audit Report 11-22, *The Federal Bureau of Investigation's Ability to Address the National Security Cyber Intrusion Threat*. Washington, DC: Government Printing Office, 2011.

National Commission on Terrorist Attacks Upon the United States. *The 9/11 Commission Report: Final Report of the National Commission on Terrorist Attacks Upon the United States*. Washington, DC: Government Printing Office, 2004.

Secretary, Department of Defense. *Establishment of a Subordinate Unified U.S. Cyber Command Under U.S. Strategic Command for Military Cyberspace Operations*. Washington, DC: Government Printing Office, 2009.

United States. *Homeland Security Act of 2002*. Washington, DC: Government Printing Office, 2002.

White House. *The Comprehensive National Cybersecurity Initiative*. Washington, DC: Government Printing Office, 2010.

———. *Cyberspace Policy Review*. Washington, DC: Government Printing Office, 2009.

———. Executive Order 13010, *Critical Infrastructure Protection*. Washington, DC: Government Printing Office, 1996.

———. Homeland Security Presidential Directive (HSPD)-5, *Management of Domestic Incidents*. Washington, DC: Government Printing Office, 2003.

———. Homeland Security Presidential Directive (HSPD)-7, *Critical Infrastructure Identification, Prioritization, and Protection*. Washington, DC: Government Printing Office, 2003.

———. *National Plan for Information Systems Protection Version 1.0: An Invitation to a Dialogue*. Washington, DC: Government Printing Office, 2000.

———. *National Security Strategy*. Washington, DC: Government Printing Office, 2010.

———. *A National Security Strategy for a Global Age*. Washington, DC: Government Printing Office, 2000.

———. *A National Security Strategy for a New Century*. Washington, DC: Government Printing Office, 1997.

———. *A National Security Strategy for a New Century*. Washington, DC: Government Printing Office, 1998.

———. *A National Security Strategy for a New Century*. Washington, DC: Government Printing Office, 1999.

———. *The National Security Strategy of the United States of America*. Washington, DC: Government Printing Office, 2006.

———. *The National Strategy to Secure Cyberspace*. Washington, DC: Government Printing Office, 2003.

———. Presidential Decision Directive (PDD)-39, *United States Policy on Counterterrorism*. Washington, DC: Government Printing Office, 1995.

———. Presidential Decision Directive (PDD)-63, *Critical Infrastructure Protection*. Washington, DC: Government Printing Office, 1998.

Internet

24th Air Force. "24th Air Force Fact Sheet." http://www.24af.af.mil/library/ factsheets/factsheet.asp?id=15663 (accessed November 19, 2012).

CISCO. "CISCO CCIE Security." CCIE Security Track. http://www.cisco.com/ web/learning/le3/ccie/security/index.html (accessed November 14, 2012).

———. "Lab Exam." The CISCO Learning Network. https://learningnetwork.cisco.com/ community/certifications/ccie_security/lab_exam?tab=take-your-lab-exam (accessed November 14, 2012).

Department of Homeland Security. "About the Department of Homeland Security's United States Computer Emergency Readiness Team (US-CERT)." http://www.us-cert.gov/about-us (accessed November 10, 2012).

———. "About the National Cybersecurity and Communications Integration Center (NCCIC)." http://www.dhs.gov/about-national-cybersecurity-communications-integration-center-nccic (accessed November 10, 2012).

Federal Bureau of Investigation. "About Us: National Cyber Investigative Joint Task Force." http://www.fbi.gov/about-us/investigate/cyber/ncijtf (accessed November 10, 2012).

———. "About Us: Quick Facts." http://www.fbi.gov/about-us/quick-facts (accessed November 10, 2012).

———. "The Cyber Threat-Part I: On the Front Lines with Shawn Henry." http://www.fbi.gov/news/stories/2012/march/shawn-henry032712 (accessed November 7, 2012).

Freedberg Jr., Sydney J. "Cyber Commands Pushing Shift from IT Workers to 'Warriors'." Aol Defense. http://www.defense.aol.com/2012/07/26/service-cyber-commands-shift-from-web-geeks-to-warriors (accessed November 19, 2012).

Fryer-Biggs, Zachary. "Panetta Green Lights First Cyber Operations Plan." Defensenews.com. http://www.defensenews.com/article/20120606/DEFREG02/306060010/Panetta-Green-Lights-First-Cyber-Operations-Plan (accessed November 7, 2012).

The Heritage Foundation. "Factsheet No. 107, Comparison of Cybersecurity Legislation." http://www.heritage.org/research/factsheets/2012/06/comparison-of-cybersecurity-legislation (accessed November 14, 2012).

Intel. "Moore's Law." http://www.intel.com/content/www/us/en/silicon-innovations/moores-law-technology.html (accessed November 10, 2012).

Lewis, Andrew. *Significant Cyber Incidents Since 2006.* Center for Strategic and International Studies. http://www.csis.org/publication/cyber-events-2006 (accessed November 19, 2012).

Lipowicz, Alice. "Huge size of DHS contractor workforce leaves senators 'astonished'." FCW: The Business of Federal Technology. http://www.fcw.com/articles/2010/03/01/dhs-has-too-many-contract-employees-senators-charge.aspx (accessed November 19, 2012).

Little, Morgan. "Executive order on cyber security builds steam amid criticisms." *Los Angeles Times.* http://www.latimes.com/news/politics/la-pn-obama-executive-order-cyber-security-20121002,0,6786970.story (accessed November 19, 2012).

Merriam-Webster. "Cybersecurity." http://www.merriam-webster.com/dictionary/cybersecurity (accessed November 4, 2012).

———. "Hacker." http://www.merriam-webster.com/dictionary/hacker (accessed November 4, 2012).

Microsoft. "Microsoft Certified Master Program." Microsoft Learning. http://www.microsoft.com/learning/en/us/certification/master.aspx (accessed November 14, 2012).

Savage, Charlie. "Private Accused of Leaks Offers Partial Guilty Plea." *The New York Times*. http://www.nytimes.com/2012/11/09/us/army-private-in-wikileaks-case-offers-partial-guilty-plea.html (accessed November 14, 2012).

United States. "Goldwater Nichols Department of Defense Reorganization Act of 1986." National Defense University Library. http://www.ndu.edu/library/goldnich/goldnich.html#97 (accessed November 14, 2012)

United States Army Cyber Command. "U.S. Army Cyber Command/U.S. 2nd Army." http://www.arcyber.army.mil/org-arcyber.html (accessed November 19, 2012).

———. "U.S. Fleet Cyber Command/U.S. TENTH Fleet." http://www.fcc.navy.mil (accessed November 19, 2012).

United States Marine Corps Forces Cyber Command. "USMC Cyberspace Update." http://www.afcea-qp.org/luncheons/31Mar11-Bullard-Cyber-Brief.pdf (accessed November 19, 2012).

United States Strategic Command. "U.S. Strategic Command History." http://www.stratcom.mil/history (accessed November 10, 2012).

———. "U.S. Cyber Command." http://www.stratcom.mil/factsheets/cyber_command (accessed November 10, 2012).

White House. "National Security Council: Cybersecurity." http://www.whitehouse.gov/cybersecurity (accessed November 14, 2012).

———. "Remarks by the President on Securing Our Nation's Cyber Infrastructure." http://www.whitehouse.gov/the-press-office/remarks-president-securing-our-nations-cyber-infrastructure (accessed November 19, 2012).

Other Sources

Center for Strategic and International Studies. *Cybersecurity Two Years Later*. Washington, DC: Center for Strategic and International Studies, 2010.

———. *Securing Cyberspace for the 44th Presidency*. Washington, DC: Center for Strategic and International Studies, 2008.

Kramer, Franklin D. *Cyber Security: An Integrated Governmental Strategy for Progress*. Washington, DC: Atlantic Council, 2010.

www.ingramcontent.com/pod-product-compliance
Lightning Source LLC
Chambersburg PA
CBHW080423060326

40689CB00019B/4361